ANOTHER MAN GONE

Kennikat Press
National University Publications
Literary Criticism Series

General Editor
John E. Becker
Fairleigh Dickinson University

Phyllis Rauch Klotman

ANOTHER MAN GONE

The Black Runner in Contemporary Afro-American Literature

National University Publications
KENNIKAT PRESS // 1977
Port Washington, N. Y. // London

Portions of this work in earlier form have previously appeared in *North Dakota Quarterly*, *American Literature*, *College Language Association Journal*, and *Studies in Black Literature*.

Manufactured in the United States of America

Published by
Kennikat Press Corp.
Port Washington, N. Y./London

Library of Congress Cataloging in Publication Data

Klotman, Phyllis R.
 Another man gone.

 (Kennikat Press national university publications: Literary criticism series)
 Bibliography: p.
 Includes index.
 1. American literature—Afro-American authors—History and criticism. 2. Afro-Americans in literature. 3. American literature—History and criticism. I. Title.
PS173.N4K55   810'.9'896073   76-18826
ISBN 0-8046-9149-5

For my parents.

CONTENTS

ANOTHER MAN GONE

INTRODUCTION

The American colonies were peopled by running men, fugitives from another continent, fugitives from justice and injustice. Some were high-minded, moral, and religious men; others were cutpurses or cutthroats. Some came to settle, others to exploit. They were as often nonheroes as men of heroic proportions, bent on adding gold and glory to the coffers and reputation of an acquisitive monarch. There were also the persecuted, people who, attempting to escape religious or political tyranny abroad, often secreted it in their own souls. Hawthorne has peopled American literature with the most memorable of these individuals, those whose psyches solidified into the immutable Puritan consciousness. Much of America's growth and stability comes from these once mobile antecedents who, having put down their roots in a new country, stubbornly refused to shake themselves free of the soil again. The majority of emigrés to America in every season have been settlers who came to stay, pioneers of one frontier. Langston Hughes lets the settler speak in his own voice:

> O, I'm the man who sailed those early seas
> In search of what I meant to be my home—
> For I'm the one who left dark Ireland's shore,
> And Poland's plain, and England's grassy lea,
> And torn from Black Africa's strand I came
> To build a "homeland of the free."[1]

The Running Man in literature is recognizable in his most simple state as the protagonist who rejects the values of the culture or society in which he finds himself by birth, compulsion, or volition, and literally takes flight. During the nineteenth century when he attempted to escape the

3

tentacles of an inimical society, he could still run away *from* but also *to* something: from the settlement to the frontier (Cooper), from slavery to freedom (the slave narrative), from land to sea (Melville), from society to the river (Twain) or to the Pond (Thoreau). Often romantic, his flight was rarely abortive. He was, then as now, a critic of his time and place. Twentieth-century society, however, in effectively depriving him of his goal, has forced his very act of running to assume complex shades of ambiguity. In order to examine these complexities in Afro-American literature, we must delineate the background of this metaphorical figure, his genesis, and his development. Spiritually he is akin to the fugitive slave, that Running Man whose desperate need was escape to freedom in or beyond the "homeland of the free."

This book establishes the presence of the Running Man in western literature and attempts to place the black runner—from the slave narrative to contemporary black fiction—within that framework. While some critics emphasize the separate and distinct qualities of Afro-American literature, the particularity of the experience, and the importance of the black folk tradition to the subtleties of the literature, this book considers Afro-American literature in the context of American and western culture and its traditions. In fact, neither approach is mutually exclusive. Sherley Anne Williams, in her thematic study of neo-black literature, makes a point about Ralph Ellison's work that seems germane to the focus of this study: he "fuses symbols from black life with symbols from Western literary tradition to create a symbolic language which is uniquely personal, yet uniquely universal."[2]

To appreciate the full range of meaning in these works, we shall discuss Afro-American literature in terms of western culture and its archetypes, while at the same time recognizing the unique themes that engage black American writers. Many of these themes persist because racism persists, for literature, as Hoyt Fuller, editor of *Black World*, has observed, rises organically out of the experience of a people. The experiences of black people in America have often called for protest; hence, a body of protest literature has developed. There was also a period which could be described as "integrationist"; then the literature took a sharp turn toward deliberate alienation and separation.[3]

Writers of the sixties began to develop their own brand of intellectual commitment to the struggle for a new and separate black ethos, with Harold Cruse as intellectual spokesman, Eldridge Cleaver as myth maker, and Addison Gayle, Jr., as enunciator of a black aesthetic. As with Emerson and his declaration of American intellectual independence more than a century ago, more and more blacks are asserting their artistic independence from the dominant white culture.

Since 1960, the work of the younger black writers has been characterized by a new awareness of the Black identity. Like the New Negro Movement of the Twenties and the Negro Revolution of the Fifties, the present Black Revolution is an effort by black Americans to clarify their identity and to determine the appropriate bases for the pride and dignity essential to the moral survival of human beings. The significant difference is that, for the first time in America, black intellectuals do not merely admit cultural differences which distinguish them from white countrymen; instead, they reject the cultural standards evolved for the white community.[4]

Because of this trend, the black critic has especially valuable insights to offer; the last section of this book is a bibliographical essay on such noteworthy black criticism.

The black writer's creative universe no longer devolves on the "Negro" as victim of white society. Black heroes today are less acted upon than acting (e.g., Tucker Caliban of *A Different Drummer* and Josh, the fighter in *Many Thousand Gone*); they are becoming the agents of their own destiny. As Running Men, they may be tricksters who dupe their white—and sometimes black—victims: Rinehart of *Invisible Man* has been followed by Reno, Mr. Jimmy, and Johnny D. of *Manchild in the Promised Land*; Rastus of *Day of Absence*; Cooley Johnson of *dem*; George Washington of *The Life and Loves of Mr. Jive-Ass Nigger*; and Bubba Handy of *Captain Blackman*, who dupes the American Army. Some, like Ben in *Coming Home* and Abe in *Captain Blackman*, completely turn their backs on America. The creators of these real and fictional characters do not seek pity or even compassion from the white reader; they address themselves more and more to the black theater audience and to the black reader. Some, like Imamu Amiri Baraka (LeRoi Jones), see the aim of the black artist as the destruction of white society, and have defined an aesthetic based on black values and black ethics.[5] Some, like William Kelley and Ronald L. Fair, use fire as the symbol of destruction brought about by the callous indifference or deliberate viciousness of the white community.

The inevitability of some kind of destruction inheres in the writings of these men. Yet in some there is a kind of pervasive optimism. They see a growing sense of unity, comradeship, and group identity, a passion for survival: the white world may become extinct but the black will not! John A. Williams's runners in *The Man Who Cried I Am* have the most hopeless outlook The good die agonizingly, if not young, with the ironically belated understanding that they have been conned to death by their own. The moral dilemma posed by the black spy-informer, a dilemma Richard Wright recognized some years ago, is now being explored in novels, in drama (including filmed drama, e.g., *Uptight*, an adaptation of *The In-*

former set in the Hough area of Cleveland), and in poetry, including Dudley Randall's "Informer":

> He shouted
> "Black Power!"
> so loudly
> we never heard
> his whispers
> to the F.
> B.
> I.[6]

    In almost all of these writers, a growing sense of rage seems to have partially displaced the frustration found in writers like Richard Wright, William Attaway, Chester Himes. In all, however, the Running Man seems to have a secure metaphorical future, or as much of a future as the Apocalypse will allow.

    This book merely opens up an area for analysis; it by no means exhausts the possibilities for exploring the symbol of the Running Man in Afro-American literature. James Baldwin and Chester Himes use the figure of the runner frequently, although only one of Baldwin's novels, *Giovanni's Room* (1956) treats it in detail. Allusions to runners in other novels offer a rich vein to mine: for example, in *Another Country* (1963), Rufus Scott is a self-destructive runner whose flight from the painful, oppressive strictures of a racist society ends abruptly when he leaps from the George Washington Bridge; and in *Tell Me How Long The Train's Been Gone* (1968), Leo Proudhammer is a peripatetic actor (Book 2 of the novel is entitled, "Is There Anybody There? said the Traveler") whose life and struggles as a black artist are extraordinarily reminiscent of Baldwin's. Chester Himes's important early work, briefly mentioned here, should be a rewarding field for future examination, particularly the novels *Lonely Crusade* (1947), *If He Hollers Let Him Go* (1945), and *The Primitive* (1955). Lee Gordon's desperately lonely crusade to cope with his feelings of isolation and fear and to find a place for himself as a man evidences the driven quality generally characteristic of the runner. He even contemplates the kind of death to which Rufus Scott finally succumbs:

There had been that deep fascination, that tongueless call of suicide, offering not the anodyne of death, but the decadent, rotten sense of freedom that comes with being absolved of trying any longer to be a man in a world that will not accept you as such.[7]

    Himes's protagonists—Robert Jones in *If He Hollers Let Him Go* and

Jesse Robinson in *The Primitive*—are both driven by their fear of oppressive white society and their consequent hate for it. Jones stops at the edge of violence; Robinson, like Wright's Bigger Thomas, does not. Richard Wright is discussed extensively in this book, but *freddaniels*, his protagonist in "The Man Who Lived Underground,"[8] can also be analyzed as a man in search of a new reality, as Ronald Ridenour suggests, whose search "must end in death because no one wishes to see *freddaniels* as he actually is nor do they want to be confronted by what he knows."[9]

Ishmael Reed's black "satanic" cowboy Loop Garoo deserves a thorough examination as a unique runner who does not fit neatly into any category. In *Yellow Back Radio Broke-Down* (1968), a novel that reverses the most valued symbols of western literature and satirizes every institution known to white society, Reed's hoodoo cowboy starts off as a circus performer—much like Bill Pickett, one of the many black cowboys who slipped unmentioned through the histories of the West.[10] After decimating the town of Yellow Back Radio (white America) and its heinous criminals, Loop rides off on his money-green horse almost, but not quite, into the sunset. Reed saves the best thrust for last. Not only do we see his hero in the American context, but we also recognize, from the moment of the Pope's arrival, that this wild Rabelaisian novel extends its boundaries to the world and ultimately to the cosmos. Loop Garoo's horse takes a mad leap and swims to the Pope's ship so that they can journey together back to where it all began.

Another body of work could be explored in this context: novels of passing. The theme of passing, as well as the role of the "tragic mulatto," has engaged both black and white writers since the nineteenth century, when masters first exercised a variation on the medieval *droit du seigneur* by appropriating the bodies of their slave women and procreating their own lighter-hued slaves. The first black novel, William Wells Brown's *Clotel, or the President's Daughter* (1853), deals with the life of the putative daughter of Thomas Jefferson and her offspring. A year earlier, Harriet Beecher Stowe's *Uncle Tom's Cabin* remarked the greater tragedy of the enslaved mulatto. Passing—flight into the white world by a person of mixed parentage, whose light skin seems to offer escape from the often gratuitous brutality of the black experience in America—has been examined by such black writers as Charles Chesnutt (*The House Behind the Cedars*, 1900), James Weldon Johnson (*The Autobiography of an Ex-Coloured Man*, 1912), Walter White (*Flight*, 1926), Jessie Fauset (*Plum Bun*, 1928), Nella Larsen (*Passing*, 1929), and such white writers as Fanny Hurst, whose melodramatic novel, *Imitation of Life* (1933), was made into two film versions, one in 1934 and one in 1959; and Sid Ricketts Sumner, from whose novel *Quality* (1946) the film *Pinky* was made in 1949. Rarely is the protagonist, whether male or female, completely happy. The flight from blackness is almost always pictured as negative and as a kind of spiritual or psychological death, but the black writer's perceptions of the complex motives and emotional pressures of the character who chooses to pass for white are inevitably closer to the truth of that experience.

Female runners include the heroines of slave escapes, like Harriet Tubman, Sojourner Truth, and Ellen Craft,[11] and the complex fictional heroines of such writers as Zora Neale Hurston, Toni Morrison, and Ernest J. Gaines. Helga Crane, the restless, self-destructive protagonist of Larsen's *Quicksand* (1928), is the antithesis of Hurston's Janie (*Their Eyes Were Watching God*, 1937), a confident, independent, black woman who takes charge of her life. Sula, in Toni Morrison's excellent novel of that name (1974), has not only the confidence and independence of Hurston's Janie but also an extraordinary intensity and individuality. Although basically not a runner, she has the mobility of mind and toughness of spirit that one associates, for good or ill, with male protagonists whose desire for freedom often sets them on the road. With Gaines's novel, *The Autobiography of Miss Jane Pittman* (1971), the slave narrative entered the 1970s as an artistic variant of the genre. The differences are obvious. Jane's flight to the North is frustrated—she never gets there. Her "birth" into freedom with a new name given her by a Yankee soldier is never completely realized. Cpl. Brown, like the North itself, holds out the possibility of freedom, but a great distance exists between the dream and the reality. Jane's journey—about one hundred years—is of epic proportions; she embodies the spirit of a people and their history of survival in America.

In answer to a question about the dominant themes in the literature of the seventies, black playwright Alice Childress responded:

"I think that all Black writers, whether they intended to or not, have been writing about not being free. Always—from the beginning of America right up to now. Of course, you find a great many white writers who have written about freedom in their own terms, but I don't think in ever so great a concentrated flood and fashion as Black writers. At least it seems to me that in any Black book, no matter what it deals with or what the story line is, you realize that the people are not free."[12]

Perhaps the reason for the frequent recurrence of the runner in Afro-American literature—from the slave narrative to the fiction and nonfiction of the seventies—is that compelling and still unrealized desire for freedom.

NOTES

1. Langston Hughes, "Let America Be America Again," in *The American Writer and the Great Depression*, ed. Harvey Swados (New York, 1966), p. 500.

2. Sherley Anne Williams, *Give Birth to Brightness: A Thematic Study in Neo-Black Literature* (New York, 1972), p. 47.

3. Blyden Jackson, in his article "A Survey Course in Negro Literature," (*College English* 35, no. 6 [March 1974]: 631-636), divides the literature into six historical periods: 1. The Apprentice Years: 1746-1830; 2. Age of the Abolitionists: 1830-1895; 3. The Negro Nadir: 1895-1920; 4. The Harlem Renaissance: 1920-1930s; 5. The Age of Wright: 1940-1950s; 6. The Black Militant: 1960-——. The last three dates are approximations I have made from the text of the article.

4. Darwin T. Turner, "Introduction," in *Black American Literature* (Columbus, Ohio, 1970), pp. 7-8.

5. See Larry Neal's "The Black Arts Movement" and other essays by black artists and critics in *The Black Aesthetic*, edited by Addison Gayle, Jr. (New York, 1971). According to Houston Baker, "Jones is an agent of apocalypse; he says he writes poems that are like bullets, and all of his work is dedicated to the destruction of white society and the creation of a new black Eden." *Long Black Song, Essays in Black American Literature and Culture* (Charlottesville. Va., 1972), p. 56.

6. *More to Remember* (Chicago, 1971), p. 71.

7. Chester Himes, *Lonely Crusade* (New York, 1947), p. 48.

8. Richard Wright, "The Man Who Lived Underground," in *Cross Section*, ed. Edwin Seaver (New York, 1944), pp. 58-102. Included in *Eight Men* (1961). Michel Fabre makes the point that the novella differs distinctly from the excerpts published under this title in *Accent*, no. 2 (Spring 1942). (*The Unfinished Quest of Richard Wright* [New York, 1973], p. 626.)

9. Ronald Ridenour, "The Man Who Lived Underground: A Critique," *Phylon* 3, no. 1 (Spring 1970): 56.

10. Pickett was featured prominently in the early 1900s program of the Moore Brothers' 101 Ranch Rodeo; he is considered the originator of steer wrestling.

11. Unfortunately, only a few women authored their own narratives; some were told-to accounts, others characterized by Arna Bontemps as "out-and-out fiction" (see Chapter I). *The Narrative of Sojourner Truth; a Bondswoman of Olden Time, Emancipated by the New York Legislature in the Early Part of the Present Century* (1850) was told to Olive Gilbert; *Scenes in the Life of Harriet Tubman* (1869) was written by Sarah Bradford; *Incidents in the Life of a Slave Girl, Written by Herself* (1861) by Harriet Jacobs under the pseudonym Linda Brent and edited by L. Maria Child. The first of the "inside the White House" stories was, however, written by Elizabeth Keckley (*Behind the Scenes; or Thirty Years a Slave and Four Years in the White House*, 1868), who was once a slave, then a modiste and confidante to Mrs. Lincoln.

12. Interview in *Black Creation, A Review of Black Arts and Letters*, eds. Jim Walker and Diane Weathers, vol. 6, Annual, 1974-75, p. 92.

1. THE SLAVE NARRATIVE:
One Hundred Years of Running

"What's wrong with running? It emancipated more people than Abe Lincoln ever did."

Ossie Davis, *Purlie Victorious*

In the slave narrative, the Running Man is in flight from bondage to freedom. A more positive goal is difficult to envision. He is running toward freedom and identity, in pursuit of a humanity denied him, in search of a state of being. All of these aspirations are clearly and specifically developed by later writers: Baldwin deals with identity; Williams with the state of being; Wright with humanity. At the same time, these later writers attest that the black protagonist's goal can never again have the simple purity of that of the runaway slave whose experiences were narrated by himself, told to others, or set down in fictionalized form over a period of a hundred years. Before we examine his narrative, however, we must consider briefly his genesis in America.

In 1526 the first black slaves were brought to North America by the Spanish. With about one hundred blacks from Hispaniola in the West Indies, these colonizers landed on the coast of what is now South Carolina to set up sugarcane plantations. But disease, to which the Indians and blacks were apparently immune, ravaged the Spaniards. An additional element, which neither the Spaniards nor other slaveholders have ever been able to eschew, was that disease symptomatic of all enslaved men—the ineluctable desire to be free. As soon as these sixteenth-century slaves found that the Indians were friendly and could guide them to freedom, they began to escape in significant numbers. Torture was used to dissuade those recaptured from again attempting such folly, but the flight to freedom continued and the colony was doomed to failure. "The Negro slaves who escaped were Americans, seventy-five years before the first settlement in Virginia."[1]

This began an inevitable sequence of painful events that contributed to the schismatic development of the United States, a country founded on a great unspoken dichotomy: freedom—for some. The desire for freedom produced the first black Running Man in America and he subsequently produced his own biography. His impulse to flee developed naturally out of his enslavement, for nothing deters a man from attempting to secure his freedom, not even the threat of brutality or loss of life. This was clearly recognized by Judge St. George Tucker of Virginia in a letter he wrote in 1800, the year of Gabriel Prosser's "conspiracy":

The love of freedom is an inborn sentiment, which the God of nature has planted deep in the heart. Long may it be kept under by the arbitrary institutions of society; but, at the first favorable moment, it springs forth with a power which defies all check. This celestial spark, which fires the breast of the savage, which glows in that of the philosopher, is not extinguished in the bosom of the slave. It may be buried in the embers, but it *still lives*, and the breath of knowledge kindles it into a flame. Thus we find there never have been slaves in any country, who have not seized the first favorable opportunity to revolt. These, our hewers of wood and drawers of water, possess the power of doing us mischief, and are prompted to it by *motives which self-love dictates, which reason justifies*. Our sole security, then, consists in their ignorance of this power, and their means of using it—a security which we have lately found is not to be relied on, and which, small as it is, every day diminishes.[2]

Judge Tucker's consternation was well founded and his caveat, that the tenuous security of the slaveholder was based on the slave's continued ignorance of his potential power, was accepted by the slaveholder but not by the slave. A glance at the number of slave rebellions recorded between 1728 and 1831 attests to that: before the colonies rebelled against England, slave uprisings occurred in Savannah, Georgia (1728); in Virginia (Williamsburg) and South Carolina (1730); in Rhode Island aboard a slave ship (1731); three in South Carolina (1739); in New York (1741); in Rhode Island (1747); in Charleston (1754); and one was contemplated in 1759. Sizable conspiracies were planned by Zamba in New Orleans in 1730; Gabriel Prosser in Richmond, Virginia, in September 1800; Denmark Vesey in Charleston, South Carolina, in 1822; and Nat Turner in Southampton County, Virginia, in 1831.[3]

One aim of these major rebellions was the annihilation of whites. Both Vesey and Turner, for example, refused to contemplate exceptions, citing the Scriptures for their rationale. Vesey insisted that "on the precedent of San Domingo, Negroes could not sustain power while 'one white skin' remained intact." Whether the conspirator was a freedman, as was Vesey, or the slave of either a vicious or "benevolent" master, the desire for revenge was always at the heart of the plan. Escape was a given. Only Denmark Vesey, however, had predetermined and apparently negotiated a plan with the government of Haiti to "receive and protect"[4] the victorious rebels. Unfortunately, no narratives were written by any of these determined and skillful conspirators. All that is extant is the told-to narrative, *The Confessions of Nat Turner* by Thomas R. Gray, published in Richmond in 1832. The avenge-and-run narrative for obvious reasons did not achieve in the nineteenth century the popularity that it has in the twentieth, and should be considered a variant of the major type.

The actual period of ex-slave literature, then, extends from 1760 (Briton Hammon's *Narrative*) to 1861 (Harriet Jacobs's *Incidents in the Life of a Slave Girl*).[5] Its proliferation, however, coincided with the abolitionist campaign (1830-1861). The abolitionists were accused of breeding the form and writing the narratives for their own propaganda purposes, and some evidence supports this accusation. Because James Williams could neither read nor write, he dictated his autobiography to John Greenleaf Whittier, whose integrity we would find difficult to impugn. But not so the editor of *The Alabama Beacon*. He insisted that Whittier had been "hoodwinked," that there was no such plantation in Alabama, although ex-slaves often used fictitious names and places in order to avoid recapture. *The Narrative of James Williams, an American Slave Who Was for Several Years a Driver on a Cotton Plantation in Alabama* was, therefore, suppressed by the Antislavery Society, which had published it in 1838, because even a hint of fraud would do their cause no good. Experiences of fugitive slaves did help immeasurably in influencing the uncommitted to join the fight against slavery. Works of doubtful authenticity do, however, exist, among which Arna Bontemps includes Charles Ball's *Slavery in the United States*, 1836. That account apparently contains some "fictionalized" truth, while others, "like Emily Pierson's *The Fugitive* and Mattie Griffith's *Autobiography of a Female Slave*, are out-and-out fiction."[6]

Genuine slave narratives, however, authentic autobiographies recalling the bondage and freedom of gifted black men and mulattoes who happened to be born under the peculiar institution, are the ones that give significance to this body of writing and justify its place in American literary and cultural history.[7]

A sufficient number of authentically documented narratives and live, articulate ex-slaves speaking aloud their experiences on the lecture platform gave the lie to their detractors. Frederick Douglass, William Wells Brown, and Henry Bibb traveled the lecture circuit with their harrowing stories for some time before committing them to paper. Gustavus Vassa, among others, wrote and published his autobiography. The ingenious methods of escape used by Henry "Box" Brown and William and Ellen Craft were so highly publicized by their well-documented narratives that Douglass admonished them for having given away valuable secrets to the enemy.

Highly respected and well-intentioned abolitionists have helped to cloud the issue by confusing fact with their own fiction. It seems fairly certain that Josiah Henson, for example, became "the original Uncle Tom" after the fact. There is no real evidence that he and Mrs. Stowe met before the initial publication of *Uncle Tom's Cabin* in 1852, yet some time after 1858 she passed the mantle to Henson and he graciously donned it:

It is difficult to determine precisely when Henson met Mrs. Stowe. Charles Edward and Lyman B. Stowe assert that the author of *Uncle Tom's Cabin* met the ex-slave in Boston in 1850. Forrest Wilson, no doubt following their lead, reiterates this statement—for which, apparently, there is not a shred of evidence. It was not until 1853 when she wrote the *Key* that Mrs. Stowe wrote the preface to the 1858 edition of Henson's autobiography. But nowhere in this book does Henson mention Mrs. Stowe![8]

A limited edition of Josiah Henson's 1849 *Narrative* was published in 1965 at "Uncle Tom's Cabin and Museum" in Dresden, Ontario, Canada. The foreword to this new edition contains the following paragraph:

The original book, narrated by Josiah Henson, is in effect, an autobiography, but it was upon facts related therein that Mrs. Harriet Beecher Stowe based her famous novel "Uncle Tom's Cabin," first produced in 1852, and since that time, reproduced in many languages and editions, so that it is universally known.

Henson's narrative has special interest because he did not become a Running Man until he had spent thirty-five or forty years in slavery. His personality has no real counterpart among the fictional or actual figures considered in this and subsequent chapters, who are without exception boys or men early disabused of the notion of accommodation or adjustment to a predatory society. Because of his preferential status and his extreme loyalty to his master (to the extent that he did *not* escape to freedom the first time he had the opportunity), Henson does in a sense deserve the now pejorative appellation "Uncle Tom." He did, in fact, bask in the acclaim which the new name gave him and which undoubtedly helped to increase the sale of his autobiography.

Sale of the slave narratives, however, was not a problem What is extraordinary, besides the proliferation of the form, is its popularity with the public. Charles Nichols gives the following sample statistics:

Gustavus Vassa's narrative went into ten editions by 1837;
Charles Ball's narrative—at least six editions issued between 1836 and 1859;
Josiah Henson's narrative—had sold 6,000 copies in 1852;
"Stowe Edition" (1888)—100,000 copies;
William Wells Brown's *Narrative* (1848)—8,000 copies by 1849;
Frederick Douglass's narrative (1845)—seven editions by 1849.[9]

Arna Bontemps compares the vogue of the slave narrative in the nineteenth century to that of the western in the twentieth:

The narratives evoked the setting and conditions of slavery, to be sure, but they also created a parable of the human condition, the fetters of mankind and the yearning for freedom. The perils of escape and the long journey toward the North Star did not grow stale with repetition until times changed and a new parable, or myth, the Western, replaced the earlier one.[10]

Yet the description of long and perilous journeys is more closely analogous to the experience of the restless frontiersman recounted during this same period by Fenimore Cooper than to the pop art westerns conceived by Zane Grey and others and disgorged onto the screen by generations of Hollywood hack writers. That Cooper created this authentic legend out of purely American materials is now a truism of literary history, but the fact that these two genres, related in a more than peripheral way, had a concomitant development during the early part of the same century has not, to my knowledge, been previously discussed. (The latest edition of Spiller and Thorp, 1969, still does not consider the slave narrative.)

Both the westerner and the slave who chose to escape were outsiders. Neither wished to be part of the dominant culture, although the westerner's lot was not forcibly inflicted upon him. He could stay and adapt to the settlement without necessarily suffering from physical deprivation, fear, or anxiety. The slave's life, on the other hand, was often in danger, especially if he made a move toward freedom. While both slave and westerner hungered for freedom, to the former it was a matter of life or death, and to the latter, life qualitatively different from that which he knew in the settlement. The westerner was in most cases a solitary individual by inclination, one who preferred the company of nature to that of society; the slave was solitary by necessity. Loneliness was a fact of existence;

lasting attachments were difficult to retain, and even familial ties were tenuous and at the mercy of the slave system. The child born into slavery was forced to be on his own at an incredibly early age. His mother may have been allowed to nurse him in the fields, but, once weaned, he was watched over by brothers and sisters or a grandmother too ancient to pick her portion in the fields. If the mother or grandmother was a cook in the big house, she was often able to "appropriate" enough food to keep the child from constant hunger. If not, he became an independent scrounger, staving off hunger any way he could—a skill put to use later when he took to the road. Frederick Douglass, who was raised by his grandmother and mentions seeing his mother only once or twice in seven years, felt a certain loss when she died, but it was not as though he were being separated from someone who had been close to him. Slavery, he affirms, destroys filial ties and alienates the individual, especially the mulatto child, from family and from the emotions of affection, reciprocal love, and loyalty.[11]

The process of alienation also resulted in many personalities characterized by hatred and aggression. Not all slaves who attempted escape were as independent and resourceful as the westerner. Many were impelled by a sudden reaction to brutality, either witnessed or experienced, or by an act of extreme ingratitude. Henson, a model slave, was horror-struck to find that his master was covertly planning to sell him South. Usually well-adjusted and calm, he suddenly felt like committing murder. On impulse, James Williams took to the road in the middle of the day after being forced by the overseer to ready himself for his own torture.

Other escapes, however, were premeditated and ingeniously executed by resourceful individuals. William and Ellen Craft planned their escape with phenomenal patience. They secreted money to buy supplies in order to make a convincing suit of male clothes for Ellen, who was almost white, and who traveled North disguised as a southern gentleman with "his" man William. Wearing a sailor's uniform, Frederick Douglass escaped by carrying forged papers and "eluding Maryland patrols to ship, Melville-like on a whaling vessel from New Bedford."[12] Henry "Box" Brown injured his finger with vitriol in order to free himself from work so that he could dream up an escape plan—one of the most ingenious and most difficult to execute. He had to fold himself into a box (3 feet 1 inch long, 2 feet wide, 2 feet 6 inches high), and stay in it for twenty-seven hours while it was shipped by freight from Richmond to Philadelphia. His ordeal was somewhat mitigated by prayer, for the escaped slave, like Cooper's westerner, was usually a religious man.

Leatherstocking had a highly individual relationship with God; characteristically, he worshiped alone, as he did most other things. The slave generally worshiped as his master decreed. However, some, like Nat Turner, were lone worshipers who reportedly had mystical experiences. Henry "Box" Brown insisted that God had answered his prayers and told him, "Go and get a box, and put yourself into it."[13]

[There were other] God-intoxicated ones: SOLOMON BAYLEY–schooled in the Bible, a nineteenth century John Bunyan, prostrate before the Almighty and SOJOURNER TRUTH–a wizened black Sybil, seeking in every Tabernacle the heavenly city.[14]

Gustavus Vassa's favorite book was the Bible; it was the book most often available in the master's house and the one which enlightened mistresses kept at hand to teach special servants.

Many ex-slave narrators could not read. We know James Williams could neither read nor write and that he told his story to Whittier. William and Ellen Craft were taught to spell and write their names by a Quaker family, the first whites to befriend them. Douglass was an exception: nothing could stop him from learning, even though his master pointed out to his mistress the folly of teaching slaves–"Keep 'em ignorant," he said, and she then obeyed. Douglass was also a deeply religious man, although he hated the hypocrisy of the church, especially that of *Christian* slaveholders–surely an oxymoron. William Wells Brown was also aware of the hypocrisy of Christian slaveholders: "Master was so religious, that he induced some others to join him in hiring a preacher to preach to the slaves."[15]

Douglass was an extraordinarily intelligent man, although not all narrators were. Williams, "Box" Brown, Moses Grandy were, like Natty Bumppo, men with a high degree of moral and physical courage and a certain amount of innate intelligence. Alone on unknown terrain or in the forest, they faced many kinds of terror and deprivation. Whereas the westerner was skilled in the ways of wood and stream, the slave very often was not. When he "lit out," his only compass was the North Star. Moses Grandy explained their plight:

They suffer many privations in their attempt to reach the free states. They hide themselves, during the day, in the woods and swamps; at night, they travel, crossing rivers by swimming or by boats they may chance to meet with, and passing over hills and meadows which they do not know: In these dangerous journeys they are guided by the North-Star, for they only know that the land of freedom is in the north. They subsist only on such wild fruits as they can gather, and as they are often long on their way, they reach the free states almost like skeletons.[16]

A "driven" quality characterizes the experience of all running men:

the escape from Europe, from law in the settlements, or from the inexorable movement of civilization westward. The most significant difference between the westerner and the ex-slave, however, is the matter of choice, and that difference has been most deleterious to the black man in his experience in America. Not having chosen of his own volition to come to this country, he has continued to have only negative alternatives. The desire for a better life with *more* freedom is different from the compulsion to grasp for freedom of any kind. And the question of penalties arises—the decision to move from the settlement to the plains did not necessarily carry with it the imminent danger of death; that risk was always implicit, however, in the black man's attempt to escape from slavery to freedom. The slave was then faced with the inevitability of retribution should he be recaptured, or the finality of death which was, under certain circumstances, preferable.

Nonetheless, we can see a kind of formula in the slave narrative that has some features in common with the story of the westerner that readers apparently came to expect. The ex-slave usually gave some background of his life in bondage, often naming names and places in spite of the risk of recapture. Some, of course, invented such details in order to protect themselves. This part of the narrative (life in bondage) was sometimes sectioned off from the escape. Henry "Box" Brown ran his narrative together in the form of an abolitionist exhortation. Frederick Douglass wrote of his bondage and then of his freedom, omitting the details of his escape. Most narrators, however, included the escape plan and its execution in a story as suspenseful as any western. William and Ellen Craft's thousand-mile trip from Macon to Philadelphia is a concatenation of harrowing events sprinkled with irony. For example, a slavetrader riding with them aboard a steamer bound for Charleston gives William's master (Ellen disguised) some "good" advice:

"I would never let no man, I don't care who he is, take a nigger into the North and bring him back here, filled to the brim as he is sure to be, with d——d abolition vices, to taint all quiet niggers with the hellish spirit of running away."[17]

William Wells Brown, when forced to become an expatriate, remarked with bitter irony: "An American citizen was fleeing from a Democratic, Republican, Christian government, to receive protection under the monarchy of Great Britain."[18] Irony, used perhaps unconsciously by these early writers, is a heritage of the black experience in America that is artistically developed by such contemporary writers as Ellison, Baldwin, Kelley, Williams, Wideman, and Beckham. This is not surprising because, as

John Oliver Killens recently wrote, "Tragedy and irony and paradox have been the core of our existence, slaves and pariahs, in the homeland of the brave and the free."[19]

William Craft included a post-escape section that gives some interesting details of northern life and its inconsistent attitude toward blacks, a phenomenon we are more apt to place in the twentieth century than in the nineteenth. After the Fugitive Slave Act was passed, the Crafts were advised by abolitionist friends to leave the country, particularly since their old masters had written to President Fillmore, who then instructed that military forces be sent to Boston to assist in their apprehension. William and Ellen Craft were among the first black expatriates in Europe, and their escape from America was a recapitulation, in small, of their escape from the South, prompting William to write:

In short, it is well known in England, if not all over the world, that the Americans, as a people, are notoriously mean and cruel towards all coloured persons, whether they are bond or free.[20]

Solomon Northup, born a freeman in New York, found this particularly true. His papers were stolen from him in Washington, D. C., and he was kidnapped and sold into slavery at the age of thirty because he was unable to prove that he was a freeman:

So we passed, hand-cuffed and in silence, through the streets of Washington—through the Capital of a nation, whose theory of government, we are told, rests on the foundation of man's inalienable right to life, LIBERTY, and the pursuit of happiness! Hail! Columbia, happyland, indeed![21]

Northup's story, a strange and terrible tale of twelve years of enforced slavery, reverses the narrative pattern while at the same time retaining all of its elements.[22]

Most of the narratives, however, follow the general pattern of bondage/escape/freedom or bondage/escape/recapture/freedom. The escape/recapture/freedom pattern recalls the artful suspense of the western, especially such blood and thunder excitement as we find in *The Last of the Mohicans*. As Spiller has noted:

For many—and this represents one real level in the book—*The Last of the Mohicans* is a breathless unrelenting chase, unbroken save when Alice and Cora are captured by Magua, and Leatherstocking, Uncas, and Duncan Hayward, thus far pursued, become the pursuers.[23]

Most slave narratives contain the pursuit theme, usually with the addition of bloodhounds—that much of Mrs. Stowe has basis in fact. Henry Bibb, who escaped and was recaptured several times, continued his forays into the South in an attempt to rescue his wife and child, with the constant threat of betrayal hovering over him. Many ex-slaves became conductors on the Underground Railroad and, like Harriet Tubman and Sojourner Truth, stole slaves out of bondage. Their route was often by water, which became a symbol of freedom for the black Running Man, as it was for Twain and Melville, and often for Cooper. Water easily swallowed up the trail of the Running Man. Nat Turner planned to have his men strike their blow for vengeance and run to the swamps, where their trail would be obscured. James Williams escaped his master's bloodhounds by taking to the water, a method dramatized in one of Leadbelly's songs, "Old Riley":

Introduction: Now this is Riley. They had bloodhounds in them times . . . The overseer in them times had a Negro named Riley. And Old Riley was one of the best there was and Old Riley was trying to make his way to freedom. And while Riley was goin', they couldn't catch up with him, and they got the bloodhounds put on his tracks and they commenced talkin' about it.

Song: Old Riley walked the water.
Old Riley walked the water.
On them long, hot summer days.
Riley walked the water,
Here, Rattler—Here.[24]

Harriet Tubman led her charges to freedom by water, and many of the spirituals she sang carried her message of freedom to the slave through the covert image of water: "I looked over Jordan, and what did I see," "Deep River."

In addition to the excitement of the pursuit, the western and the slave narrative share the characteristic of violence and death. Cooper describes various kinds of torture and death peculiar to Indian culture, as well as the kinds of violence perpetrated by the white man outside the law of the settlement. One of the most vivid chapters in *The Prairie* is devoted to the Old Testament sentence and execution of Abiram White by his brother-in-law, Ishmael Bush. Slave narrators describe in excruciating detail their often terrible lives of intermittent violence, violence committed against either themselves or their fellow slaves. The overseer, a special breed of sadist, was usually the perpetrator of violence. William Wells Brown writes of having seen his mother flogged by the overseer Cook.

Frederick Douglass describes, with some objectivity, the brutality and murder (sometimes accidental) which he witnessed, pointing out that such actions were *not* confined to overseers. He saw some masters and mistresses run amok, proof to him that slavery corrupts and erodes the honest emotions of white and black. Moses Grandy reports that widowed slaveowners often hired professional whippers to keep their slaves in line. Henry "Box" Brown, a slave near Richmond, Virginia, reports having seen slaves cut down, whipped, hanged or half-hung, apparently in retaliation for the revolt of Nat Turner. James Williams, a driver under a white overseer (Huckstep) on his master's plantation in Alabama, witnessed floggings of men and women who were unable to keep up during the cotton picking season. His most horrifying description is of a pregnant woman who was tied to a tree face forward and beaten by Huckstep until she delivered a dead infant.

Violence and death were permanent partners in the slave system. Their threat bred surface docility but engendered repressed fear and hatred, which often erupted into real aggression. Slaves, in their impotent fury, struck out at each other and at themselves when they could not escape from or retaliate against their oppressors. Solomon Northup, continually harrassed and threatened by his master, turned on him and whipped him with his own whip. In a state of uncontrollable anger, Douglass struck an overseer. The psychology of the slave system bred an atmosphere of incipient violence. "Everybody in the South," Douglass wrote, "wants the privilege of whipping someone else. The whip is all in all."[25] Some slaves refused to be flogged and became special challenges to the overseer. Both Grandy and Williams tell of two heroic slaves who were killed but not subdued by the whip. Rare was the happy, contented slave, if he ever, in fact, existed. The singing, shuffling "darky" was a masquerade staged for "massa." Behind the mask was very likely a man ready to run and kill, if necessary, for his freedom.

The Running Man of the slave narrative is a heroic figure in Afro-American literature and an illustrious part of black tradition, although unfortunately not yet a part of the mainstream of American tradition. He proves that the spirit of freedom never deserted the black man, even though he endured the most appalling conditions of servitude. The hardships he faced as slave, and later as fugitive, have been documented impressively by Charles Lyell, Frederick Law Olmsted, Harriett Martineau, Charles Dickens and others; yet his own record provides more insight into the complexity of the Running Man and his psyche than we can get from reams of objective evidence. And men they were. They ran from slavery because they were not recognized as men; they had, in fact, no identity, sometimes not even a name. William (Wells Brown) was forced to relinquish his Christian name because the master's son was also named William.

After his final escape, having been recaptured once, he wrote, "I was not only hunting for my liberty, but also hunting for a name."[26] An old Quaker who helped him when he reached Ohio told him, "Since thee has got out of slavery, thee has become a man, and men always have two names."[27] Hence, he became William Wells Brown, the man Arna Bontemps calls "the first creative prose writer of importance produced by the Negro race in America."[28]

The literary importance of the narratives, according to black historian John Blassingame, lies in the tradition they bequeathed to future black writers:

The growth in black novels, poetry, prose, historical works, and drama can be measured roughly by the increasing literary merit found in the black autobiography. The few well written antebellum autobiographies, indicative as they were of the lack of literary skills and traditions (indeed, even literacy) in the black community had few parallels in *belles lettres*. On the other hand, the relatively high quality of the autobiographies written after the war presaged Corrothers, Charles W. Chesnutt and Paul Lawrence Dunbar, and finally burst forth in the Harlem Renaissance.[29]

A line of influence can be drawn from the slave narratives to the best works of twentieth-century literature, from the pre-Harlem Renaissance novel, *The Autobiography of an ex-Coloured Man* (1912) by James Weldon Johnson to the fine historical novel by Ernest J. Gaines, *The Autobiography of Miss Jane Pittman* (1970). Besides forging a link in the tradition of black literature, the slave narrative has been:

one of the major forums of black protest, a chief source of accurate historical information . . . . From Frederick Douglass to Malcolm X, Samuel Ringgold Ward to Richard Wright, Gustavus Vassa to H. Rap Brown, William Wells Brown to Eldridge Cleaver, the central theme has always been the same: a demand for freedom from the enslavement of the body, mind, and soul.[30]

NOTES

1. Nicholas Halasz, *The Rattling Chains; Slave Unrest and Revolt in the Antebellum South* (New York, 1966), p. 2.
2. Joshua Coffin, ed., *An Account of Some of the Principal Slave Insurrections* (New York, 1860), p. 30.
3. Ibid. p. 10.
4. Halasz, *Rattling Chains*, p. 133.

5. Charles H. Nichols, *Many Thousand Gone: The Ex-Slaves' Account of Their Bondage and Freedom* (Leiden, Netherlands, 1963), p. 203. (Now available in paperback, Indiana University Press, 1969).
6. Arna Bontemps, "The Negro Contribution to American Letters," in *American Negro Reference Book*, ed. John Preston Davis (Englewood Cliffs, N.J., 1966), p. 864.
7. Ibid., p. 865.
8. Nichols, *Many Thousand Gone*, p. 141.
9. Ibid. pp. xiv-xv.
10. Bontemps, "Negro Contribution," p. 867.
11. Frederick Douglass, *My Bondage and My Freedom, Part I—Life as a Slave, Part II—Life as a Freeman* (New York, 1855), p. 60.
12. Nichols, *Many Thousand Gone*, p. 2.
13. Henry "Box" Brown, *Narrative of the Life of Henry "Box" Brown, Written by Himself*, first English edition (Manchester, 1851), p. 43.
14. Nichols, *Many Thousand Gone*, p. 2.
15. William Wells Brown, *Narrative of William Wells Brown, An American Slave, Written by Himself* (London, 1849), p. 36.
16. Moses Grandy, *Narrative of the Life of Moses Grandy, Late a Slave in the United States of America* (Boston, 1844), p. 28.
17. William Craft, *Running a Thousand Miles for Freedom: or The Escape of William and Ellen Craft from Slavery* (London, 1860), p. 49.
18. William Wells Brown, *Narrative*, p. 120.
19. John Oliver Killens, "The Confessions of Willie Styron," *William Styron's Nat Turner: Ten Black Writers Respond*, ed. John Henrik Clarke (Boston, 1968), p. 34.
20. Craft, *Running*, p. 111.
21. Solomon Northup, *Twelve Years as a Slave; Narrative of Solomon Northup, a Citizen of New York, Kidnapped in Washington City in 1841 and Rescued in 1853* (London, 1854), p. 64.
22. "The major hazard was not escape from the plantation (which had no locked gates or barbed wire), but the journey beyond. Outside the plantation, the fugitive faced patrollers armed with rifles and assisted by dogs . . . . Beyond the patrollers, the fugitive must travel on foot without compass or map across a thousand or more miles of strange country where he or she might be stopped by a suspicious white or betrayed by a black. Traveling by night, hiding by day, the fugitive hoped that the land or some kind person would provide food or drink until he or she reached the journey's end in a place called Canada . . . . When one considers the difficulties and the dangers, it is not surprising that a Solomon Northup planned escapes for ten years without attempting any; in fact it is amazing that any slaves fled." Darwin T. Turner, "Uses of the Antebellum Slave Narratives in Collegiate Courses in Literature," paper given at the Midwest Modern Language Association Meeting, St. Louis, Mo., November 1, 1974.
23. Robert E. Spiller et al. eds., *Literary History of the United States*, 3rd ed. (New York, 1963), p. 263.
24. Moses Asch and Alan Lomax, eds. *The Leadbelly Songbook* (New York, 1962), p. 38.
25. Douglass, *My Bondage*, p. 72.
26. William Wells Brown, *Narrative*, p. 98.
27. Ibid, p. 105.
28. Bontemps, "Negro Contribution," p. 868.
29. John W. Blassingame, "Black Autobiographies as History and Literature," *Black Scholar* (December 1973-January 1974): 9.
30. Ibid., p. 9.

2. THE ARCHETYPAL RUNNING MAN IN THE LITERATURE OF WESTERN CIVILIZATION

Without visible antecedents, the figure of the Running Man began to appear in the first narratives written by escaped American slaves. We cannot postulate or even suggest a direct connection, yet this archetypal figure is well known in the literature of western civilization. Odysseus and Oedipus were seekers, Orestes a fugitive, Cain and Ishmael wanderer-outcasts. The runner's origins were often noble or mysterious; he could be a criminal or a hero, and at times was both. He often had a destiny to fulfill of which he may or may not have been aware (Orestes, Aeneas), a sin to expiate (Cain), or a penance to serve (the Wandering Jew, the Ancient Mariner, the Flying Dutchman). Medieval romance is replete with the quest theme: a knight searching for the Holy Grail, as in the Arthurian Legends, or off on some wondrous journey, like Sir Gawain or Spenser's Red Cross Knight; or an unacknowledged heir seeking his throne (Havelock the Dane, Bevis of Hampton).

The pilgrimage tradition set noble and ignoble alike on the road to the Holy Land or to more accessible shrines like Canterbury. Shakespeare tells us that even Henry IV planned a penitential trip to the Holy Land after the unfortunate yet timely death of his cousin Richard. The literary role of the pilgrim continued beyond the days of Chaucer and Shakespeare to the pilgrimage of the English Puritans to America and the allegorical pilgrimage of Bunyan's Christian Everyman to the Celestial City. The soul in search of salvation did not begin its journey with Dante's *Inferno* in the fourteenth century and will probably not end with the *Hell* of Imamu Amiri Baraka in the twentieth.

Runners do not always seek salvation. Some are seekers of knowledge, others fame; some freedom, others power; some wealth, others identity ("Who is it that can tell me who I am?"). The quest of Don Quixote in the seventeenth century differs from that of Rasselas in the eighteenth. The former sought a glorious past, the latter a way of life for the future. And yet the shabby gentleman of La Mancha and the Prince of Abyssinia have something in common, which they share with Voltaire's peripatetic traveler, Candide. All take to the road with a companion whose presence is a comment, by contrast, on the runner and his quest. In their travels, Rasselas and Candide, born on paper only a few days apart, express the inherent skepticism of two extraordinarily different thinkers in an age of superficial optimism. Neither finds in his search for wealth, power, or a philosophy of life an answer outside himself, or, as in the case of Rasselas, an answer without the help of a benevolent deity.

The criminal runner, on the other hand, is not bothered by philosophical or religious considerations. Jack Wilton, Nashe's Unfortunate Traveler, is the apparent father of the English rogue-runner and criminal biographer, whose wild adventures usually bring him, not the the gallows, but to fortune, fame, and the female of his choice. The original picaro, however, has continental roots: Lazarillo de Tormes in Spain and Gil Blas in France. The picaro's antecedents are often as mysterious as Oedipus's (Humphrey Clinker, Joseph Andrews, Tom Jones), and his quest for wealth, although tinged with criminality, is enhanced by a character as wily and cunning as Odysseus's (Roderick Random, Peregrine Pickle, Moll Flanders—the female picaroon).

Odysseus is at times a cunning and artful escapee, as was the American slave when he propelled himself onto the road. But he is "Noman" by guile, not a "nonman" (the role Richard Wright has attributed to the black man, whom he calls "a kind of negative American")[1] by virtue of dehumanized bondage. The Running Man has a number of archetypal characteristics that can be traced through the various stages of western literature: the Greek and Roman classics, the Bible, the pilgrimage convention of England, Germany, and France, the picaresque tradition of Spain, France, and England, and the travel tale common to the literature of most countries in the western hemisphere. These characteristics usually have to do with the motive for running and the agent's role as seeker, wanderer, outcast, or fugitive.

The questing runner—Odysseus, who knows he has a goal to reach; Oedipus, compelled to search for his identity; Aeneas, for whom the gods have a divine plan; Orestes, who seeks revenge—is often of royal lineage and heroic dimensions. Unlike the later rogue-runner's, his quest is rarely related to the acquisition of wealth. And even though it may take years, he persists until his goal is realized. When Oedipus first sets out upon the road, he knows he is of royal birth and that, in effect, the road "belongs" to him. When he asks Creon to banish him and blindly totters from Thebes, he cannot see the road but he *can* see himself. He has fallen from high estate, but his search for identity has been realized; no longer a king, he is still a hero. In the next stage of his flight, however, he takes on the characteristics of the penitential seeker, and we can see in him portents of the wanderer-outcast.

Odysseus, on the other hand, is the prototype of the seafaring adventurer; his destination is Ithaca and Penelope, yet his wanderings open some of the marvels of the universe to him, the kind of marvels that have for centuries lured the sailor to the sea. Some of the earliest Anglo-Saxon poetry (e.g., "The Seafarer" from *The Exeter Book*, ca. 725 AD) reflects this irresistible urge. Tennyson has the older Ulysses hungering after his earlier peripatetic life, his questing spirit undaunted by age or infirmity; Melville's Ahab has qualities of the dauntless Homeric seafarer, as do Conrad's adventuring seamen. Aeneas takes to the sea, not as victor returning home, but as a man in flight for his life. His adventures open up the marvels of the ancient world to him, but his quest, like that of the runaway slave, is for a "promised land." His journey, however, is guided by the gods and, with tenacity and courage, he eventually reaches his goal and fulfills his destiny.

Interestingly, Aeneas's travels have not lent themselves to the kind of parody, burlesque, or creative variants that Odysseus's travels have prompted—although Chaucer does mention Aeneas not too kindly in the *Legend of Good Women*. Lucian's parody of the *Odyssey* fathered not only Fielding's *Journey from This World to the Next*, but that great mythic journey, *Gulliver's Travels*. *A True Story* is a tall-tale-travelogue which includes fantastic storms at sea, epic battles, and a delightfully ironic incident in Hades, in which Odysseus slips Lucian a note to deliver to Calypso while Penelope's back is turned. The godlike heroes of the ancient world are reduced by Lucian to the size, not of Lilliputians, but of mere men— the kind we see much later in Joyce's Dublin during Leopold Bloom's peregrinations.

The travel tale received new impetus when the great explorations began in the fifteenth century. Those who couldn't make the dangerous trip to new and exotic lands were transported by the diaries of travelers and by travel accounts both real and fictitious. The intrepid voyager facing the dangers of unknown lands and the unknowable sea became the knight errant of the New World. His real adventures inspired writers to create fictional counterparts in drama, poetry, and later, in the novel. Byron's *Don Juan* stemmed in part from the adventures of his grandfather, "Foulweather Jack," whose *Narrative* was published in 1768; Coleridge was familiar with James Cook's accounts of three of his Pacific voyages (1777) and with Shelvocke's *Voyage Round the World* (1726) when he wrote the *Ancient Mariner*; Cowper had read about the voyage of the Centurion before he wrote *The Castaway*. Stories of the survival of shipwrecked victims were current in England as early as 1610 (e.g., *A Discovery of the Bermudas*); we know that Shakespeare put three such travel accounts to use in writing *The Tempest*.

The intrepid traveler metamorphosed into tenacious survivor is epitomized by Robinson Crusoe, whose tale, based on the experiences of Alexander Selkirk, is an epic of endurance. Having lost the power to pursue his own course, he is forced into an aloneness akin to that of the biblical Ishmael, whose plight is due for the most part to conditions over which he has little or no control. Crusoe sees himself as a kind of Cain-wanderer, although the religious element in Defoe is not strong. William Bligh's *Narrative* (1790) is an account of mutiny and enforced suffering at sea not unlike that of Robinson Crusoe on land. No longer a voyager and adventurer, the Running Man becomes a victim, and like the runaway slave, he elicits admiration and sympathy because of his indomitable spirit. After his distasteful experiences Gulliver *chooses* to isolate himself, to become a fugitive from mankind; he becomes a victim of his own misanthropy, not of something outside himself. The nonvolitional runner, on the other hand, is manipulated by circumstances or, as in the case of Orestes, by destiny and the gods.

Orestes is a questing runner, but with far less volition than other classical runners. Like the infant Oedipus, he is in a sense banished from his home and later forced to avenge the death of his father, for which he must then atone. For much of his life he is driven by revenge and then hunted and harried by the Furies. His ultimate quest is for redemption, for expiation of a sin he was compelled by the gods to commit. Orestes has little of Oedipus's pride, Odysseus's cunning, or Aeneas's courage. He does not exert the same kind of will as they do, and in this sense he is more like the biblical fugitive-outcast.

Cain and the Wandering Jew are condemned to a life on the run, both having committed sins against God or God's laws. (Ishmael's "crime" is of another sort; he's a bit like the mulatto child, the unwanted progeny of master and slave who must be cast out in order to preserve the stability of society.) The Cain figure in later literature—in Byron's Mystery Drama, for example, is not simply the traditional outcast-fugitive. More than a mere criminal, he is a man set apart from others by a questing spirit, one to whom "knowledge is good / And life is good; and how can both be evil?"[2] True to the *Genesis* account, Byron's Cain is banished, destined to wander in the wilderness, marked against the easement of death with that special mark unknown except to those who would have vengeance wreaked upon them sevenfold were they to slay him. The Wandering Jew in various accounts is also recognizable, not by a special mark but by his appearance and his actions: old, gaunt, and white-bearded, he is almost always penniless but very often does good deeds without accepting payment of any kind. Always he remains an enigma to those whose lives he touches.

Other Romantics, including Coleridge, Wordsworth and Shelley, were attracted to the theme of the Wandering Jew. The Mariner, unlike Byron's Cain, does not seek truth or knowledge. His crime against nature makes him a penitential outcast whose road is harsh and endless; though penitent, he is doomed to eternal wandering and loneliness. According to Maud Bodkin, John L. Lowes demonstrated some years ago (*The Road to Xanadu*, 1927) "that the figure of the Mariner in the mind of Coleridge merged or interpenetrated with that of the Wandering Jew, Cain, and perhaps also a sea wanderer, Falkenberg—a variant of the Flying Dutchman."[3] Wordsworth, in his "Song of the Wandering Jew," makes the Wanderer a symbol of frustration; penitent like the Mariner, he too is doomed to seek but never to find salvation. On the other hand, Shelley's Ahasuerus (*Queen Mab*) is presented, according to Joseph Gaer, "as a Jewish Promethean character who defies the Lord and suffers perpetually but remains unrepentant."[4]

The English poets were not alone in their fascination with the symbolic figure of the Wandering Jew. He appears in the literature of almost every country in Europe.

But the Germans, more than any other peoples, were fascinated by the legend and its implications, and they have created the greatest body of poetry on the topic. From the end of the eighteenth century to the beginning of the twentieth century, almost every major and minor poet in Germany, directly or indirectly, coped with the symbol of the Wandering Jew.[5]

Apparently even Goethe had planned a poem of epic proportions in which Ahasuerus was to be a symbol of Reason and Christ a symbol of Faith.[6]

The Wanderer also appears in German and French fiction of the nineteenth century: Oelkers, *Princess Mary of Oldenoff, or The Wandering Jew*, 1848; Schücking, *The Peasant Prince*, ca. 1851; Alexander Dumas, *Tarry Till I Come: or the Everlasting Jew*; Eugene Sue, *The Wandering Jew*, 1844. According to Gaer, Sue's Wanderer is a symbol of "restless and exploited humanity,"[7] while Dumas's Laquedem is a man who, having wandered for fourteen centuries, cursed with immortality for his sin of pride, finally receives divine grace through repentance and the intercession of the Pope.

Both *The Phantom Ship* (1831) by the Englishman Frederick Marryat and Wilhelm Hauff's "ghostly ship" story in *The Caravan* were well known in Wagner's time, but there is no proof that he'd read either before writing his opera, *The Flying Dutchman*. According to Ernest Newman, Wagner, in *A Communication to my Friends* (1851), "describes the legend of the Flying Dutchman as a blend of that of Ulysses and that of the Wandering Jew."[8] Wagner's Dutchman is in a way an ironic blend of the seafaring adventurer and the wanderer-outcast. The Dutchman's bold and questing spirit leads him unwittingly into the latter role, but it is Satan, not Christ, whom he offends.[9] For his audacity, Satan condemns him to another kind of Mariner's life-in-death: eternal and watery wandering, mitigated only by a respite on land every seven years. Like many reluctant wanderers, he has attempted to do away with himself, but (unlike the Wandering Jew) his only hope for salvation is through, not divine intervention, but the love of a faithful woman.

For the most part, however, women play a secondary role in the life of the Running Man. One of his major characteristics is his solitariness, his inability or reluctance to make permanent attachments. The runner, like the traditional hero as Lord Raglan describes him, is usually alone: "We find him miles from the nearest habitation, often with a sword, sometimes with a horse, but never with any spare clothing or any provisions for the journey. His lack of provision never causes comment, though his loneliness is explained in various ways."[10] Some examples Lord Raglan gives are from the literature of ancient Greece:

Odysseus, having lost all his companions at sea, travels through the wilds of Ithaca to attack single-handed his wife's suitors. Oedipus is travelling alone when he meets and kills his father, King Laius, who is accompanied only by a charioteer.[11]

Orestes's flight from the Furies is all the more painful because he is alone. The biblical wanderers are alone because they are outcasts not only from the society of men but also from God's grace, alone with their real or assumed guilt. Early peoples may have developed the idea of the mythic wanderer because society tended to cast out the sinner against its taboos. Certainly, as the legend of the Wandering Jew passed from culture to culture, the one characteristic he seems to have retained is his guilt. He is guilty of doubt, of audacity, of defiance, of the inordinate desire to know.

Another characteristic of many runners is the desire to question the meaning and purpose of existence, a desire that often places them in conflict with society's rules. "The authority against which people in a primitive society revolted often became symbolized in the father or Father."[12] The first man set the stage for the inevitable father-son conflict and for subsequent banishment or flight. The desire of youth to seize its place or to know too much too soon has been the basis for contention between the generations for centuries. The struggle may be interpreted as the aspiration to godhead; more often it is the aspiration to manhood, an ingredient in the revolt of the slave (always called "boy") against the master. Telemachus sets out on his journey not simply to find his father but also to find himself. Stephen Dedalus (*Ulysses*)[13] does much the same thing centuries later, although the significant aspect in *Portrait of the Artist as a Young Man* is the rejection of authority epitomized by the church and the church fathers. Boswell's *Journals*, especially the London *Journals* not found until this century, reveal a young man fleeing to the city to escape from parental authority. Byron, "The Pilgrim of Eternity," in truth and in poetry was in constant flight from authority of various kinds, as was his friend, E. J. Trelawney. And Mahon's (man's) flight in *The Playboy of the Western World*, after the ostensible murder of his father, is surely symbolic of that stage in the life of every man when he rejects, either peaceably or forcibly, the authority of the father and asserts his independence.

Young men who wish to abjure the beliefs of their fathers, to seek out their own identity as individuals, or to turn their backs on society's restrictions and conventions have almost always been running men at some time in their real or fictitious lives. Whether they take to the sea or to the road, [14] they are usually restless and unafraid, or shrewd enough to hide their fears. Sometimes leaders, they are rarely followers. If they seek the material things of this world, they usually learn quickly how to adapt to the rigors of the road. Some, like the picaro, are skilled in shape-shifting maneuvers, disguises, and aliases. If they have a mission to accomplish, a penance to fulfill, or a goal to reach, they are zealous, inspired, selfless, and able, if not always willing, to suffer both mental and physical hardships.

The Running Man in the literature of western civilization is not always young, but he is invariably endowed with a special spirit. For good or ill he is set apart from other men, in some degree, by his ability to endure. If he has chosen to unfetter himself from the bonds of society and to seek freedom, he may suffer pain but also joy in his quest. And if he reaches his goal, in this world or another, he has completed the journey that is to the reader a symbol of man's ability to prevail.

NOTES

1. Richard Wright, *White Man, Listen!* (New York, 1957), p. 40.
2. George Gordon, Lord Byron, *The Works of Lord Byron*, ed. Thomas Moore (London, 1833) XIV, 20.
3. Maud Bodkin, *Archetypal Patterns In Poetry: Psychological Studies of Imagination* (London, 1948), p. 55.
4. Joseph Gaer, *The Legend of the Wandering Jew* (New York, 1961), p. 121.
5. Ibid., pp. 113-114.
6. Ibid., p. 116
7. Ibid., p. 123.
8. Ernest Newman, *Stories of the Great Operas and Their Composers* (Garden City, New York, 1928), p. 287.
9. Baraka obviously had in mind his own ironic twist to the legend of the "Dutchman" when he bestowed that title on his first play. Lula, the white female who tries verbally to destroy the young black man, Clay, and then stabs him to death, is apparently white society's traveling subterranean executioner. After the subway riders (society) dispose of Clay's body, Lula continues to travel the train awaiting her next black victim.
10. Lord Raglan, *The Hero: A Study in Tradition, Myth, and Drama* (New York, 1956), p. 270.
11. Ibid., p. 271.
12. Gaer, *Wandering Jew*, p. 150.
13. Kermit Frazier suggests that Cecil Braithwaite, in John Wideman's novel, *Hurry Home* (1970), somewhat resembles Stephen Dedalus in his interest in language. Cecil *is* in exile, seeking a father ("the castle, the home, the father, the seeking"). He embarks on a journey with Charles Webb (perhaps a Leopold Bloom, but certainly "Mr. Charlie," the white man whose culture is a monument of deceits and a web of lies), a writer who is in exile searching for the son he has fathered by a black woman. Cecil's quest takes him through Europe (western culture) and then to Africa: it is a symbolic journey back through the racial past, "But it is more the past of a whole people for he is an educated Black man vague about a sense of himself, but who goes imaginatively to Black culture in search of a much more solid base." ("The Novels of John Wideman, An Analysis," *Black World* [June 1975] : 33.)
14. Ray and Banjo (Jake turned sailor), each for his own reasons, take to the road *and* to the sea in Claude McKay's novels *Home to Harlem* (1928)—see Chapter IX—and *Banjo* (1929). Jake/Banjo knows boxcars as he knows ships and his way around the edges of America, as well as the "Ditch" of Marseilles. Neither a searcher nor a questioner, Banjo is a sailor-minstrel as the name implies, a kind of black picaro, who loves life and is at ease in it, secure in his black identity. He is juxtaposed to introspective Ray, who seeks restlessly yet energetically to find himself as a black man and a writer.

3. THE RUNNING MAN IN AMERICAN LITERATURE: Nineteenth Century Background

In American literature the Running Man is a tradition, an important fictional figure reflecting one facet of our national character. From Cooper's *Prairie*, in which we can see what Richard Chase calls "the escape from culture itself"[1] embodied in the figure of Natty Bumppo, the metaphor of the Running Man can be traced through Thoreau, Whitman, Melville, Twain, and Fitzgerald to such contemporary writers as Updike, Salinger, and Kerouac. This and subsequent chapters will attempt to show the Running Man's incipient beginnings, his unique development by individual black writers, and his relationship to the mainstream of American life and letters. It is difficult, if not impossible, to compare the experience of the Afro-American with that of any other race or group that has come to this country of its own volition. An effort will be made, however, to illumine the unique aspects of the black experience in America through the manner in which various black writers embody that experience in the Running Man. This character draws his life from the earliest narratives written by escaped American slaves, as well as from the main current of American literature.

The Running Man metaphor has four strands leading into the twentieth century. Although not mutually exclusive, they can be categorized as follows: running as an inward exploration, an expansion of the self (Thoreau and Whitman); running as escape from society and identity (Natty Bumppo, Ishmael, Huck Finn); running as a criminal activity (Ishmael Bush and the confidence man); and finally, running as literal escape from physical bondage (the fugitive slave), a category also applicable to some early whites.

RUNNING AS INWARD JOURNEY OR EXPLORATION [2]

This category includes the two men who spent most of their creative lives delving into themselves. Each has written a major work so highly individualistic as to defy classification. Thoreau's explorations concentrated almost exclusively on the life of the mind, while Whitman considered himself poet of the body as well as the soul. Whitman's inward search is celebrated in "Song of Myself." The object of his quest, like that of Thoreau, is the self, but he differs from Thoreau in his mode of expression and also in the size of his voice.

Whitman is Rabelais to his own Gargantuan self: "I am large. . . . I contain multitudes."[3] Like some smiling, benign Moloch, he swallows all of America and spews it out in acres of verse that are a paean to the self. He is all things thought, felt, or seen, all things human or divine: the "hounded slave," the "mashed fireman with the breastbone broken," an "old artillerist," man and woman, good and evil. "I become any presence or truth of humanity here." Whitman projects himself imaginatively into all life. The metaphor of the journey is for him not a movement into the self to escape society, but a reflection of his leviathan attempt to "explore" and "become" humanity through the self. As Fiedler so aptly puts it:

[Whitman's] essential mythology is derived from his own personal experience, lived or dreamed, and his hero is, therefore, himself. He is, in this sense, the first truly modern poet with epic ambitions, the first author to portray himself as the mythic representation of his people and his time. His Odysseus is Walt Whitman, his Descent into the underworld, the plunge into the darkness of his own mind.[4]

Both Thoreau and Whitman must, of course, be considered symbolic runners. Thoreau was a pioneer of the westward frontier of the mind— "The frontiers are not east or west, north or south, but wherever a man fronts a fact"[5] —an explorer of the self who had no need to travel far in order to put the world by. Thoreau's answer to the question of what the West stands for is to show that the frontier of one's own mind is a far better place to travel: "Explore your own higher latitudes," he says. "Nay, be a Columbus to whole new continents and worlds within you, opening new channels, not of trade, but of thought."[6]

Thoreau's running has two aspects: first, the desire to escape the conventions of a materialistic society, that "nervous, bustling, trivial Nineteenth Century,"[7] and second, the compulsion to "search for the buried life of the soul."[8] Not until Thoreau was able to absent himself from civilization could he become wholly immersed in nature, the real locus of action for the mind. Then he could commence his real life's work, the exploration of the self.

Charles Anderson, in his excellent work, *The Magic Circle of Walden*, reads *Walden* as a poem which

reveals itself as an experience recreated in words for the purpose of routing the World altogether and discovering the Self. Its real theme is the search for perfection. (Anderson 1968, 17)

He also points out quite correctly that Walden Pond was certainly not in the wilderness, that it was indeed

only a mile and a half from Concord, a town of two thousand inhabitants. Within sight was the well-traveled highway to Lincoln, and across the pond was the Fitchburg Railroad. But the topography presented in Walden has only tenuous connections with Massachusetts. The pond, with the one-room hut on its shore, lies at the center of a symbolic landscape. (Anderson 1968, 64)

Clearly, we are dealing with a cerebral runner, one who is actually standing still in every way except the most significant. His uncharted path cannot be traveled in exactly the same way by any other, and his destination (the ideal self), if ever reached, can be the source not only of inner satisfaction but also of ineffable joy, the kind that comes from self-knowledge and spiritual plenty. J.A. Christie discusses Thoreau's symbolic journeying in detail, but one fact stands out: the exploration of oneself "through an exploration of the natural world . . . its natural features and its human environmental phenomena together" is as characteristic of Thoreau as his "preservation of truth through paradox," in *Walden*, his "account of a traveler's stay in one place."[9]

Whitman was often a desultory traveler from job to job and place to place, rusticating on Long Island when he wanted to escape New York. He is above all a symbolic traveler in "Song of Myself," in which he lets the self expand in the pure ether of freedom. Thoreau, the mind-traveler, settles into his own symbolic landscape and also creates his own conditions of isolation and solitude. In this he foreshadows later runners, like Ellison's Invisible Man, who constructs a fanciful retreat by "burrowing" underground with his mind. Both of these running men divorce themselves from the world for a time, yet both are reborn into it. Each describes his rebirth in the characteristic voice of his own century:

You think I am impoverishing myself by withdrawing from men, but in my solitude I have woven for myself a silken web or *chrysalis*, and, nymphlike, shall ere long burst forth a more perfect creature, fitted for a higher society.[10]

I'm shaking off the old skin and I'll leave it here in the hole. I'm coming out, no less invisible without it, but coming out nevertheless. And I suppose it's damn well time. Even hibernations can be overdone, come to think of it. Perhaps that's my greatest social crime, I've overstayed my hibernation, since there's a possiblity that even an invisible man has a socially responsible role to play.[11]

The question of social responsibility plagued Thoreau most of his life. In *A Week on the Concord and Merrimack Rivers* he struggles with the dichotomy in his own nature between the active and contemplative life. Theoretically, he could recognize a certain efficacy in the tension set up by the pull of these opposite poles. Actually, he seemed to experience more than a little discomfort from the frequency and intensity of the attraction to both. Like a child emotionally split by loyalty to two parents, he was drawn, not always gently, to one and then the other. When he eschewed society, the quarrels of men and states, politics, newspapers, and unctuously zealous abolitionists, he was happier:

It is a great pleasure to escape sometimes from the restless class of Reformers. What if these grievances exist? So do you and I.[12]

He could always use his pursuit of self-perfection to rationalize his withdrawal from action. "The reform which you talk about can be undertaken any morning before unbarring our doors" (Thoreau 1906, 131). The contemplative life was deeply rooted in Thoreau's nature and he seems to have maintained this part of himself inviolate, even after the return from Walden Pond, by continuing his forays out of society as a Walking Man.

Although much more of a city man than Thoreau, Whitman was also a walker. Richard Chase describes him as a "humorous loafer, principled bathtaker, saunterer, sage."[13] It seems unlikely that Thoreau would place Whitman in his special "Walker Errant" category; Thoreau was too purposeful a walker. Sauntering was a serious business to him, a crusade into the Holy Land of the mind. Thus he was not a permanent fugitive but a man who could move in and out of society when he chose to or needed to, living a kind of border life between nature and society. Most running men, as we shall see, are outsiders who occupy a kind of neutral ground or No Man's Land at some point in their lives.

Whitman, although gregarious at times, was in many ways the outsider as artist. As Chase notes:

There is much evidence to convince us that he gave people the impression of living outside the usual order of things, related to but different from the world of ordinary men. . . . This peculiar estrangement from the world is one of the striking facts about Whitman.[14]

Whitman's alienation, his failure to "adjust" to society, may have finally been the reason for the emergence of his poetic talent as it manifests itself in "Song of Myself."

His power of fantasy would allow him to escape into an innocent, regressive, Eden-like realm and it would also allow him symbolically to assault and overwhelm a world of ordinary reality which had proved to be, on its own terms, too much for him. He would utterly escape and defy the world's attempt to establish in his shifting psychic economy a super-ego—to impose upon him this or that conventional "identity."[15]

What is eminently clear is that both Whitman and Thoreau were opposed to society's restrictions on the individual and, like most running men, resisted society's conventional identities. Whitman's public masks are as numerous as his poetic ones, his many divergent selves in "Song of Myself."

He invented not one but several public personalities—the worldy, dandified young metropolitan journalist of the early 1840's; the homely Christ-like carpenter and radical of the early 1850's; the full-bearded, sunburned, clean-limbed, vigorously sexed, burly common man of the later fifties and early sixties; the male nurse and good gray poet of the Washington period; the sage of Camden of the late years.[16]

Thoreau also had many selves. Anderson calls attention to the protean nature of the "character" Thoreau invents for himself in *Walden*. Taking up Moldenhauer's discussion of Thoreau as the *eiron* of traditional comedy (his Concord neighbors functioning as different types of the *alazon*), Anderson points out that

one of the most attractive aspects of the *eiron* is his shape-shifting skill. . . . In a country of self-made men, like America, where great emphasis is put on one's occupation, it is particularly effective satire for the vocationless Thoreau to take on this Protean guise, slipping into and out of fanciful versions of all the trades and professions.[17]

It is worth noting that the touch of the ironist can be felt in most creators of the nineteenth-century Running Man, with the possible exception of Cooper. In addition, the runner's protean guise is a characteristic we will see developed and expanded to another dimension by Melville and the twentieth-century heirs of the confidence man.

One other aspect of Whitman's running should be considered. In "Song of Myself," where he "loafes and invites his soul," there is no outward movement; the motion, as we have noted, is all inward. In "Song of the Open Road," however, the self journeys along a never-ending road, escaping from all that is restricting and limiting:

Afoot and light-hearted, I take to the open road,
Healthy, free, the world before me,
The long brown path before me, leading wherever I choose.[18]

The road is freedom. In Whitman's democratic vision, it is open to all—the felon, the diseased, the beggar, the black, the escaped youth:

Like the opening pages of *Moby Dick*, like *Huckleberry Finn*, and the early chapters of *Roughing It*, and like such lesser works as Frost's "The Lone Striker," "Song of the Open Road" is a celebration of free will, a confident assertion that whatever happens one can always (as Huck Finn says) "light out for the territory."[19]

In Whitman then we have another strong link to the twentieth-century Running Man, as well as an ineradicable kinship with Thoreau, Melville, and Twain.

RUNNING AS ESCAPE FROM CONVENTIONAL IDENTITY

Escape from conventional identity, also applicable to Thoreau and Whitman, is central to the concept of running in Ishmael, Huck, and Natty Bumppo. Ishmael is the first American wanderer in the Odysseus mold. He embodies the romantic nineteenth-century adventurer who pushes away from the known, the restricted and boundaried land, and seeks after a wider range of knowledge—the infinite, the profound—the sea. Going to sea is the abandonment of his conventional identity. Huck and Natty Bumppo are motivated by a similar impulse: they run to escape from the roles assigned them by society, by the town and the settlement. Ishmael was at one time a schoolmaster, he tells us—like Melville himself, Thoreau and Whitman—an identity which none was loathe to relinquish, for it is a landlocked calling, and land is monotony, conformity, restraint. The sea is mystery and possibility:

"How I snuffed the Tartar air—how I spurned the turnpike earth!—that common highway all over dented with the marks of slavish heels and hoofs; and turned me to admire the magnanimity of the sea which will permit no records."[20]

To some critics, Ishmael's impulse is self-destructive, a desire for final escape. According to Newton Arvin, "the sailing of the *Pequod* is to be for Ishmael a temporary passage out of existence."[21] But Paul Brodtkorb sees Ishmael's "itch" to get to sea as an escape from

that mood in which land encompasses the familiar, the boring, the super-ficial, the static, the deadly, the too definitively formed, because the sea provides the elemental contrast with the land.[22]

The strange is always present at sea, but so is the terrible. Ishmael says, "Consider once more the universal cannibalism of the sea; all whose creatures prey upon each other, carrying on eternal war since the world began" (Melville 1964, 364). Brodtkorb characterizes this sea-world as al-most completely masculine. "Such a world sheltering such creatures is predominantly masculine rather than feminine, hard rather than soft." [23] One significant characteristic of the Running Man, as we will see with Huck, Natty, and others, is his compulsion to escape the feminine world, or at least that aspect of it which represents any restriction of his freedom. Women and marriage have no part in Ishmael's life (and no significant part in Ahab's). Even the mother in Ishmael's life is not "real," and his memo-ries of her are significant only in that she was instrumental in introducing him to some of life's inexplicable terrors. The world to which this American Odysseus escapes may be fraught with perils both seen and unseen, know-able and unknowable, but it is activated by the masculine principle and is singularly free of those feminine snares encountered by his famous Achaean predecessor.

Ishmael's past is foggy. We know he has a stepmother and a father, now deceased, and a name which he appears to have assumed casually for his role as narrator. According to Brodtkorb, and the point is well taken:

[The] name is equivocally stated, despite the abruptly imperative form of its declaration. The narrator precisely does *not* say that his name *is* Ish-mael; or even that he is called Ishmael, as a kind of nickname.

Simply, "Call me Ishmael." We are left to conclude that the narrator, "for reasons of his own, would rather not say who he really is."[24] The equivo-cal manner puts a certain amount of distance between us and the narrator as it does in *Invisible Man*, in which Ellison's narrator assumes not a name, but namelessness, as he tells his tale. Because a name is withheld, the nar-rator (in both cases) remains to some extent a stranger. Unlike Natty

Bumppo, whose various appellations are *bestowed* upon him, Ishmael and the Invisible Man *take on* names, which become, like the transparencies of Smollet or Dickens, eminently appropriate to their character or calling. Ishmael has had several unsatisfactory vocations on land: he has been a country schoolmaster, a "stone-mason, and also a great digger of ditches, canals, and wells, wine-vaults, cellars, and cisterns of all sorts." We also know him as a storyteller—"the first and continuing guise in which he presents himself"[25] —a sometime sailor and a wanderer. He embodies the protean aspect of the Running Man as well as his characteristic restlessness. Ishmael temporarily enters into a kind of creative unity with his fellow man aboard the *Pequod*, but he is essentially a stranger, as his assumed name suggests, an outsider, and "a traveler *through* the world."[26]

Like Thoreau, Ishmael abandons the highway and strikes out on uncharted paths. He is in a sense father to those later runners—the expatriates, Wright's Fishbelly, Baldwin's David (*Giovanni's Room*) and Williams's Harry Ames (*The Man Who Cried I Am*), who want desperately to escape the identity to which they are inevitably wed in America. At the end of *The Long Dream*, Fishbelly "sits on a plane winging his way from the known, the restricted, the fearful, toward what is unknown, less restricted, and hopeful." [27] Another continent may mean another identity, or at least the striving toward a meaningful sense of self.

The voyage of the *Pequod* means for Ishmael the abandonment of his individual identity and the assumption of a new sense of humanity— "It's a mutual joint-stock world, in all meridians" (Melville 1964, 93). At some point during the voyage he comes to identify himself with all men. Ashore he has already become blood brother to Queequeg, the uncorrupted pagan whom he unwittingly signs on to the vessel of a corrupt Christian world. Aboard, he signs on for the mad voyage to which the crew commits itself:

I, Ishmael, was one of that crew; my shouts had gone up with the rest; my oath had been welded with theirs; and stronger I shouted, and more did I hammer and clinch my oath, because of the dread in my soul. A wild, mystical, sympathetic feeling was in me; Ahab's quenchless feud seemed mine. (Melville 1964, 239)

After this he identifies increasingly with Ahab, with his cause, his monomania, and his doubt. Yet Ahab is finally revealed to Ishmael as a man totally alienated from the human community. "It is fitting that he [Ishmael] should be the sole survivor since he is the only man aboard who sees Ahab's monomania in its true light."[28] The Running Man, usually by virtue of being an outsider (Brodtkorb also calls Ishmael a "voyeur"), is able to glimpse the reality behind the protagonist's mask. He is also changed by this knowledge or his course significantly altered: Ahab's tragic error sets Ishmael on his permanent course as wanderer, compelled to live out the tragic consequences of the voyage. In general, the Running Man is the speaker, who shares his revelation with us. This is true not only in *Moby Dick* (Ishmael-Ahab), but also in *The Great Gatsby* (Nick-Gatsby), in *On the Road* (Sal Paradise-Dean Moriarty), and in *The Man Who Cried I Am* (Max-Harry Ames).

The ability to identify with others seems to be one facet of the Running Man's character. He can step outside of himself and empathize with other men, enter into a kind of imaginative unity, as Ishmael does with the men of the *Pequod* ("we were one man, not thirty") and with Queequeg in what Newton Arvin calls a "creative dependency of fraternal emotion." [29] Natty Bumppo is able to identify with the hunted and harried, and with other outsiders—not just the Indian but also Ishmael Bush, the squatter-outcast. Huck identifies in a limited way with Tom and in a much more meaningful sense with Jim. Yet he retains his objectivity. By the end of the book, Huck sees *through* Tom Sawyer's mask of tomfoolery, but he allows him to continue the charade. Both he and Jim, the two escapees from society, have invested in a human relationship that stands outside and above the moral order represented by Tom Sawyer, and certainly above the chivalric code Tom has adopted from English romance. For this reason they are able, with an inordinate amount of patience (particularly on Jim's part), to allow Tom to ring down the curtain. This is fitting because Tom has a permanent role in the social scene, while Jim has been denied an acceptable identity and Huck has refused his. The two outcasts join forces, and gradually reveal themselves to each other: no longer fugitive orphan and runaway slave, they become part of a larger humanity, the fraternity of Everyman which Ishmael joined at sea. Huck and Jim join this fraternity at the river, a symbol of freedom to Twain's fictional fugitives, and Huck takes his new commitment to freedom of conscience (in the lap of that river) seriously. According to R. W. Stallman, the river supplies "the central purpose of representing conscience, spiritual integrity, the baptismal source for rebirth and self-recognition of true identity."[30]

Huck refuses to abandon his new identity for society, to be petted and cajoled into "sivilization," even though Jim is happy to remain and assume his new identity, that of a free man. For essentially nothing is changed. The townspeople are still the same; slavery still exists, although its strictures have been somewhat ameliorated in Jim's case; Tom is still acting out his bookish tales, trying to shape reality into romance; and Huck himself is still as much a prey for do-gooders as he was before Pap's death. What's more, Huck's conversion is real. Once he has gone to hell, his commitment is permanent. How can he be a good and moral Christian now that he has rejected the values of the sanctified? Huck can no more return to the town than Natty Bumppo can return to the settlement, so he "lights out for the Territory," the domain of the old westerner.

In nineteenth-century America, it was still possible to eschew the trappings of civilization by physically absenting oneself from its more virulent forms. At a time when the American frontier still existed, Fenimore Cooper cast the classic mold for the fictional Running Man—the westerner, fleet of foot, "quick on the draw and immune to guilt."[31] Arna Bontemps has compared the success of the slave narrative in the nineteenth century with that of the western in the twentieth. But the twentieth-century western is in fact an offspring of Cooper's Leather-Stocking series (the striking similarities between this genre and the slave narrative have already been discussed in Chapter I).

Cooper's Running Man is a maverick, an outsider by choice who stands in the No Man's Land between the Indian and the white communities acting as chorus, commentator, and critic of both. Natty's flight from culture is also a flight from the conventional, static identity foisted on him by society. On the prairie and in the woods he has numerous appellations— Leatherstocking, Deerslayer, Long Rifle, Pathfinder, Hawkeye—which, in the manner of Indian tribal custom, reflect his abilities, and allow him to assume different identities commensurate with his changing self-concept. Cooper saw himself as a critic of American life, but nowhere is he more effective in his criticism than when he speaks through Natty Bumppo (*The Prairie*), aged into the old trapper, who explains to Ishmael Bush why he left the settlement:

"They scourge the very 'arth with their axes. Such hills and hunting grounds as I have seen stripped of the gifts of the Lord, without remorse or shame! I tarried till the mouths of my hounds were deafened by the blows of the chopper, and then I came west in search of quiet. It was a grievous journey that I made; a grievous toil to pass through falling timber and to breathe the thick air of smoky clearings, week after week, as I did!"[32]

Yet even America comes to an end. By the time Natty dies he has come to the last frontier. By the time Kerouac's Running Man sets out on the road, the frontier, along with the westerner, has totally vanished (for the generation of the beatific, the road itself becomes the end). The Vanishing American was red-skinned warrior as well as white westerner; both were fated to die with the frontier. The Indian was himself a Running Man, although not by choice. The old trapper, however, runs because he refuses to stand still while the rapacious white man levels the country.

"It will not be long before an accursed band of choppers and loggers will be following on their heels, to humble the wilderness which lies so broad and rich on the western banks of the Mississippi, and then the land will be a peopled desert, from the shores of the main sea to the foot of the Rocky Mountains; filled with all the abominations and craft of man, and stript of the comforts and liveliness it received from the hands of the Lord." (Cooper 1912, 215)

Natty Bumppo remains an outsider to his last breath. He never compromises with civilization by returning to the settlement. Not even the blandishments of Middleton or Paul Hover can alter his decision; he is obdurate to the end.

"Settlements, boy! It is long sin' I took leave of the waste and wickedness of the settlements and the villages. If I live in a clearing, here, it is one of the Lord's making, and I have no hard thoughts on the matter; but never again shall I be seen running willfully into the danger of immoralities." (Cooper 1912, 433)

Nothing could be clearer than the pivotal position of the westerner in Cooper's saga of western expansion. An outsider, he stands with his face to the West, able to appreciate, at an almost atavistic level of awareness, the primitive innocence of the Indian and the primeval beauty of the untouched wilderness. At his back is the inexorable movement of civilization, with all its contradictions: culture and avarice; refinement and rapaciousness; progress and plunder. Actually, Leatherstocking belongs to neither camp. An exile from the clearings, he has passed beyond the line of demarcation and, responsible only to himself and his Christian consciousness, he is able to assume a kind of middle-ground objectivity from which to comment.

No matter what we think of the ingenuousness, the infantilism of the great innocent of American fiction, he has survived apparently because he reflects something deeply rooted in our national character. Perhaps he represents, in the romantic tradition, not what we were but what we wished to be. Perhaps it is simply the desire to be free, unfettered, unconstrained; the desire *not* to adjust, *not* to accommodate, *not* to belong: alienation by choice. Harry Angstrom and Chig Dunford share this motivation, as does Holden Caulfield, to some extent. Leatherstocking, however, chose to be a Running Man at a time in our history when he could still escape to the wilderness. He expressed his disapproval of the "waste and wickedness of the settlements" by turning his back on them forever, "in order to live where he may at any moment look up to God and maintain the spotless purity of his life."[33]

Laugh as we may at the assorted breed he has fathered, our great respect for Cooper's original westerner is based on his courage, independence of belief and action, personal loyalty and bravery under fire, and his support of the hunted and harried. His role as Running Man critic is ambiguous because we can see in it his deficiencies as a man, for the runner, regardless of his purity of motive, is by nature one to whom immobility is anathema, one who cannot for a variety of reasons be satisfied to remain in the clearing, in the town, or on the shore. He is rarely interested in or capable of committing himself to long-term relationships, especially with women. Neither Ahab nor Ishmael, for example, has the capacity for heterosexual love, as Newton Arvin points out.[34] Indeed, Fiedler suggests that the protagonists whom we identify as running men are actually

in flight from woman and home. Cooper's Natty flees the settlements and the prospect of marriage with squaw or paleface maiden; Melville's Ishmael rejects his cruel step-mother and the whole world of security she represents; [and] Twain's Huck evades all the women who try, with rigor or gentleness, to redeem his orphaned state.[35]

We can, with almost the same results, carry this trend through the twentieth century: Holden Caulfield, "Rabbit" Angstrom (a classic example of flight from home and family), Dean Moriarty, Ellison's Invisible Man, Kelley's Chig Dunford, Calvin Hernton's "Scarecrow." There are exceptions; Tucker Caliban *(A Different Drummer)* is one, Ishmael Bush another, and several fugitive slaves, such as William Craft, who included their wives in their escape. Nevertheless, enduring heterosexual relationships remain the exception for the Running Man, including Thoreau and Whitman, those two great explorers of the self.

Instances may be found of strong friendships between men, what Fiedler calls the "homoerotic relationship"[36]—Natty Bumppo and Chingachgook, Ishmael and Queequeg, Huck and Jim, "Rabbit" and Tothero, Dean and Sal Paradise. Except for the latter two, however, the relationships mentioned last only as long as the dramatic incident itself, and then the Running Man is again on the move *alone*. His lifestyle precludes a continuing relationship with man or woman, and his own nature dictates his special kind of narrowed existence. He may be brave, resourceful, and loyal, but he is incapable of committing himself to love. Principles, struggles—yes; friendship perhaps, but not love. He is above all independent, an outsider whose shifting environment is scarcely conducive to family life. Conceivably, this denial of the normal male emotional and sexual drive gives added impetus to the Running Man's impulse to flight. Relationships tend to restrict his mobility, to make him adjust or at least accommodate, to deny him his most precious possessions, solitude and independence. Fiedler adds one real and one fictional runner to his category of runaways:

[Alexander] Henry and Natty and Rip together constitute the image of the runaway from home and civilization whom we long to be when we are our most authentic selves; Dame Van Winkle and Hannah and Eve add up to the image of his dearest enemy, spokesman for the culture and the European inheritance he flees.[37]

The Running Man suffers, then, from a kind of arrested development in relationship to women. He tends to think in terms of absolutes, to look for perfection, to move from one encounter to another, or to avoid women completely. In general, he eschews the company of most men also, preferring nature (Thoreau, Natty, Huck) or his own solitude ("Rabbit," Chig Dunford, Ellison's Invisible Man). The Running Man is usually wary of confiding in or placing his trust in others. Accustomed to relying on himself, he is reluctant to rely on anyone else and is highly circumspect with strangers. His lack of expansiveness may be the natural outcome of a solitary existence, but for the next group to be considered, reticence is often a necessity for survival outside the law.

RUNNING AS A CRIMINAL ACTIVITY

For nineteenth-century fictional characters such as Ishmael Bush and the confidence man, running is a form of criminal activity, an escape from the law, without the impulse toward human freedom that motivated the slave to escape from bondage. Theirs is basically an anarchic, self-interested detachment from the group. However, the juxtaposition of Ishmael Bush and Natty Bumppo in *The Prairie* dramatizes the unresolved tension in Cooper's own attitude toward the westward movement of civilization and the men who spearheaded that movement. Which *is* better, civilization or nature? If we are to believe, consistent with Cooper's social theory, that civilization's vices are far outweighed by its potential benefits, then the ultimate death of the brave and great-hearted warrior and the eventual leveling of the land are a part of the ultimate good. Leatherstocking must be viewed as outsider and critic but also as a part of the passing parade. How then are we to view Ishmael Bush: as arch-villain, scapegoat, a necessary stage in the evolution of the western frontier? The dichotomy in Cooper's thinking makes it difficult to reach any facile conclusion. One thing is clear—the means by which the ultimate goal of civilized refinement is reached are highly questionable.

Ishmael Bush and his criminal brother-in-law, linked by collusion, are part of the inexorable process of civilization, unheroic outsiders who press into the wilderness and appropriate land they consider theirs by God's law, not by society's proscriptions. The squatter tells Leather-stocking:

"I am as rightful an owner of the land I stand on, as any governor of the States! Can you tell me, stranger, where the law or the reason is to be found, which says that one man shall have a section, or a town, or perhaps a county to his use, and another have to beg for earth to make his grave in? This is not nature, and I deny that it is law. That is, your legal law." (Cooper 1912, 64-65)

Yet the trapper identifies and sympathizes with the squatter in opposing society's restrictions, for they both seem "ultimately to deny the whole idea of society."[38]

"I cannot say that you are wrong," returned the trapper, whose opinions on this important topic, though drawn from very different premises, were in singular accordance with those of his company, "and I have often thought and said as much when and where I believed my voice could be heard." (Cooper 1912, 65)

Significantly, the old trapper shows the squatter and his family the best places to encamp, thereby sharing guilt for their profanation of the wilderness:

"I might have knowed it—I might have knowed it! Often have I seen the same before; and yet I brought them to the spot myself, and have now sent them to the only neighborhood of their kind within many long leagues of the spot where I stand. This is man's wish, and pride, and waste, and sinfulness!" (Cooper 1912, 92)

Although Ishmael Bush's activities are illegal, unlike the confidence man, he behaves illegally out of principle—it is civil disobedience on a tribal level. Having no use for society, he lives on the "skirts" of the settlement in a kind of primitive subculture (of his own making) that attempts to be totally self-sufficient. What he resents most is interference with his freedom to live where and how he wants and to take what he needs, unimpeded by law, lawmakers, and law-enforcers:

"The air, the water, and the ground, are free gifts to man, and no one has the power to portion them out in parcels. Man must drink and breathe, and walk, and therefore each has a right to his share of 'arth. Why do not the surveyors of the States set their compasses and run their lines over our heads as well as beneath our feet? Why do they not cover their shining sheepskins with big words, giving to the landholder, or perhaps, he should be called the airholder, so many rods of heaven, with the use of such a star for a boundary-mark, and such a cloud to turn a mill?" (Cooper 1912, 86-87)

Opposed in principle to "legal" settlement, Ishmael and his tribe continue to wander, outcasts from society; yet, ironically, they actually spearhead the movement of civilization into the prairie. In some ways their role is strangely analogous to that of the Sioux, a tribe known for its treachery. The comparison is implicit in Chapter IV where Cooper first introduces the Indians who have captured Natty, Paul Hover, and Ellen Wade:

The unfortunate bee-hunter and his companions had become captives of a people who might, without exaggeration, be called the *Ishmaelites of the American deserts.* [My emphasis.] (Cooper 1912, 39)

Paul Hover is incensed at being captured, but he pretends to see some possible advantage to Ellen and himself if the predatory Sioux were to fall upon the squatter and his party:

"If they will carry the *tribe of wandering Ishmael* to the Rocky Mountains," said the young bee-hunter, laughing in his vexation with a sort of bitter merriment, "I may forgive the rascals," [My emphasis.] (Cooper 1912, 40)

What the Sioux are to their prairie neighbors, Ishmael Bush, the borderer, and his tribe are to the settlers who live within the law. Both tribes are essentially migratory, both parasitic and willing to subsist on what they can appropriate; both have leaders who are proud and unremitting in their anger, courageous, yet suspicious and vengeful. Cooper sets the two Ishmaelite tribes side by side on the prairie where they act alternately as enemies and uneasy allies. Clearly he wants to identify the lawless white man with the miscreant Indian, his most effective method of persuading the reader that both cultures breed outcasts and that the complicity of the lawless portends inevitable defeat.

Yet there is much to mitigate the harshness of Cooper's judgment against Ishmael and his sons. Paul Hover reluctantly acknowledges their courage and their skill with a gun:

"Few men love Ishmael Bush and his seven sledgehammer sons less than one Paul Hover; but I scorn to slander even a Tennessee shot-gun. There is as much of the true stand-up courage among them, as there is in any family that was ever raised in Kentuck itself. They are a longsided and double-jointed breed; and let me tell you, that he who takes the measure of one of them on the ground, must be a workman at a hug." (Cooper 1912, 41)

These semi-barbarous people are at their best when facing violence and death. Ishmael is proud that Asa died as a son of his should die, "a dread to his enemy to the last, and without help from the law" (Cooper 1912, 163). But his death cannot go unavenged, even if it means cutting out the murderer from their own flesh. Therefore, in spite of the fact that Ishmael brings with him into the wilderness some highly questionable "benefits" of civilization—criminal indifference to nature, acquisitiveness, murder, justice without mercy—Cooper allows him a certain patriarchal dignity and surely the most striking scene in the book, the Old Testament judgment of Abiram White. Ishmael's intense anguish when he is compelled to avenge his son's death is depicted by Cooper with extraordinary insight and sensitivity. Cooper's treatment of this side of the old squatter indicates that he never fully resolved the troublesome and ubiquitous issue of the cult of nature versus the cult of civilization. The borderer is endowed with a sense of pride and dignity at the end of *The Prairie* that we could scarcely anticipate from his introductory description:

[Ishmael Bush] boasted that he had never dwelt where he might not safely fell every tree he could view from his own threshold; that the law had rarely been known to enter his clearing; and that his ears had never willingly admitted the sound of a church bell. His exertions seldom exceeded his wants, which were peculiar to his class, and rarely failed of being supplied. He had no respect for any learning, except that of the leech; because he was ignorant of the application of any other intelligence than such as met the senses. (Cooper 1912, 71)

The borderer is in almost every way the antithesis of that paragon of the prairie, Natty Bumppo. Yet, as one critic says, "the Bush family at least know how to take care of themselves and have a kind of dignity. In their company Leatherstocking too has dignity."[39] Natty and Ishmael represent two types of running men. Both are escapees from the clearing, but the borderer is apparently more representative of those who spilled out of the settlement onto the prairie and opened the frontier. According to Cooper, such men were unrestrained because they were beyond the law, brave because they were inured to danger, proud because they were independent, and vindictive because each was the avenger of his own wrongs (Cooper 1912, 70).

Ishmael Bush and his tribe of borderers are to some extent the expendables of the westward movement, just as the Cross Damons are the expendables of contemporary society. Richard Wright's Outsider, like Cooper's, considers himself beyond the law, morally unrelated to society's values. Unresponsive to its rewards or punishments, he sees himself as both judge and executioner—the rationale of the borderer who actually found himself alone in the wilderness.

The wanderer-outcast may be a not unusual peripheral type, a by-product of any movement of civilization or progression of society, the anarchic element in the struggle for change. Nat Turner, along with other black rebels against slavery, is a Running Man who shares with Ishmael Bush the compulsion to exact retributive justice outside the law; he also harbors an unshakable conviction that he is God's agent on earth. Ishmael Bush has no such conviction—he uses the Bible, which he cannot read, as a source book of suitable punishments and a rationale for their execution. Ishmael's manipulation of God's order and man's law is purposeful and unrestrained. Nor is he inhibited by the thought of consequences. In fact, he ceases to run *not* because of external pressure or fear of legal reprisal, but because of dissension from within. What drives Ishmael back to the settlement is the perfidy of his wife's brother and its aftermath. He does not think in terms of adherence to a code of conduct required by society, or one that is self-imposed, like Leatherstocking's, which Cooper enunciated earlier in *The Pioneers*. George Dekker points out that what the action of that novel "reveals again and again is that Leatherstocking's conduct is governed by a code which is far more strict and demanding than any devised by Judge Temple."[40] Society's code, devised by the lawmakers, is replaced in the wilderness by Natty's code of the woods, which, as Richard Chase says, "entails skill in the lore of the hunt, honor in personal conduct, piety toward nature, stoic forbearance, a sort of programmatic masculinity, and celibacy."[41] Such a code is clearly inimical to the law-skirting, criminally inclined borderer who is, in fact, far more representative of the frontier "type" than is the magnificent old trapper who meets his Maker on the prairie.

Criminal activity is developed and refined by Melville in the figure of the confidence man, one of those outgrowths of civilization with which Cooper did not deal, but who nonetheless followed the frontier as it moved westward. The confidence man has the guile and cunning which the borderer lacked, in addition to a protean skill for disguise and dissimulation. Melville developed this character at a time when he himself was suffering from a sense of personal alienation and disaffection, when he had lost confidence in the existence of a moral order in the universe. Just after he had finished writing *The Confidence Man* he had his despairing conversation with Hawthorne. As Hawthorne described it, Melville was unable to believe or to be comfortable in his unbelief, and *The Confidence Man* surely reflects this quandary. Melville had experimented earlier with this fictional breed. The "Lightning-Rod Man" was a purveyor of panaceas, a Running Man who sold his meretricious product in times of fear and anxiety, for the confidence man flourishes in an atmosphere of distrust and disillusion. Melville's most complete examination of the type, however, is in *The Confidence Man,* in which he places his protean character aboard the *Fidèle* on its way down the Mississippi on April Fools' Day. The book is a satirical masquerade acted out on the *Fidèle,* itself a fantastic Mardi Gras afloat, appropriately bound for New Orleans with its cargo "of that multiform pilgrim species, man."[42]

The figure of the confidence man, which Melville appropriated from folklore, was, Richard Chase tells us, already composite:

He embodied the Yankee and the Westerner. On the popular stage in the decades immediately preceding Melville's book, the peddler had merged into the figure of Brother Jonathan, who came gradually to be presented in a striking costume: flaxen wig, white bell-crowned hat, blue coat with long tails, red-and-white trousers. Finally, the Yankee peddler had become Uncle Sam.[43]

Because of his humorous folk background, the confidence man has been viewed with a certain amount of affectionate indulgence, stemming not only from the patriotic ambience surrounding the figure of Uncle Sam, but also from our complacent satisfaction in seeing P. T. Barnum's axiom in action. Clearly, the confidence man demands full confidence of his dupes. The Lightning-rod Man fails because the householder puts his confidence in God, not in man; the confidence man succeeds aboard the *Fidèle* because mankind is less and less able to make moral choices in a seemingly godless universe. Like the tragic hero who acquiesces in his own demise, the con man's dupe is a party to his own deception. We see it over and over again: the sickly old miser who cannot resist another speculation and even begs to be bilked again by the con man in the guise of herb-doctor; the student with his superficial knowledge who is easily outsmarted by the Agent of the Black Rapids Coal Company with its headquarters on the Styx. Even Pitch the frontiersman, who seems insulated against the blandishments of the confidence man, is finally "undone when the con man appeals to his vanity and his latent kindliness."[44] It is for little enough, but Pitch knows it for the devil's trick, and he becomes "an Ishmael," another Melvillean outcast.

The confidence man, like the wanderer-outcast, functions on the edge of society. He stings the conscience or the pocketbook and runs. Melting into the crowd and escaping at the next port, he is rarely around long enough to be found out. Whether a mute of questionable purity or a counterfeit Guinea, he appears only long enough to fool or dupe or gull the crowd. Yet he always has a successor, for the ship of fools never runs aground. Melville eliminates much traditional frontier or riverboat humor found in the tellers of tall tales, the trickers and practical jokers of Thomas

Bangs Thorpe, J. J. Hooper, and later, Twain. The practical joke in *The Confidence Man* is played on the whole human race and Melville's black humor antedates the contemporary brand by almost a hundred years. The confidence man is one side of Everyman and on Melville's ship, moving into darkness, he leads himself to his own conclusion.

Although not exclusively an American phenomenon, the confidence man has certainly spawned with ease in our waters. He is almost as familiar a figure in American literature as Cooper's mythic westerner; he is perhaps more familiar in American life, for he "still dwells in the land." Although he plied his trade in the old West, he also fared well as a Yankee peddler in the East. He could sell patent medicine and cstealls from a covered wagon at the roadside, peddle gadgets in his Yankee "get-ups," and do his sleight-of-hand tricks on a Mississippi gambling boat. The secular Tetzel of the nineteenth century—goods hawker and moral trapsetter for the guilty-hearted—he is probably "cousin-german" to the traveling salesman, so much a part of the American scene and the American joke in our not-too-distant past. Today he sells "guaranteed" used cars, permanent youth, and healthful filter-tips. He is the political panderer to offshore oil interests, the drug pusher, the hustler, the numbers runner. His mask and his product may change from time to time, but his salient characteristics are permanent: he is smooth-tongued and quick-footed, a Running Man who is also a master of guile.

A concomitant development of the confidence man tradition in America grew out of slavery and the plantation system, and is especially germane to the development of the black Running Man in American literature. Arna Bontemps has examined the "familiar trickster theme" in Afro-American folklore in his Introduction to *The Book of Negro Folklore*. The trickster's name was usually Jack or John, and if he succeeded in gulling "Old Massa" or "Old Miss" or even the Devil, it was always by his wits.[45] A distinct relationship exists between this character and Calvin Coolidge Johnson, the con man in William Melvin Kelley's novel, *dem* (1967).

The slave who could outwit his overseer or master found his life less terrible and his burdens less onerous. If he knew how to dissemble, he could talk himself out of work, out of trouble, and into a good meal. Most ex-slaves whose narratives were examined in Chapter I report that their lives often depended on their ability to fool the white man. Spirituals sung by seemingly ingenuous slaves carried escape messages lyrically past the ears of the unsuspecting slaveowner and helped many a fugitive cross "over into camp ground." Until he was able to take to the road, however, the slave learned to fool or dupe his master by putting on a face that the master wanted to see: the happy, shuffling "darky" with the ubiquitous grin, memorialized by the minstrel show, was the first black confidence man.

Ellison's B. P. Rinehart in *Invisible Man* is a descendant of this dual American tradition. He has almost as many masks as Melville's confidence man: he is "Rine the runner and Rine the gambler and Rine the briber and Rine the lover and Rinehart the Reverend,"[46] and he dupes both black and white. His shape-shifting skill is exceeded only by his fast footwork and his facility with the word:

BEHOLD THE INVISIBLE!

The old is ever new
Way Station in New Orleans, the home of mystery,
Birmingham, New York, Chicago, Detroit, and L. A.

No Problem Too Hard for God. [47]

Some twenty years before *Invisible Man*, a black confidence man appeared in George Schuyler's satirical novel, *Black No More* (1931). Max Disher, whitened into Matthew Fisher via Dr. Crookman's "black-no-more" method, becomes one of America's classic con men. He not only cashes in on racism, served up by the "Knights of Nordica," but through some of his antics and the color-cure treatments, many profiteers from political racism suddenly find themselves out of business.

An even more sophisticated black confidence man—the black spy—. was later developed by Richard Wright out of his observations of CIA activities during the height of the Cold War. In a speech at the American Church of Paris, he described

the means by which the dominant white society in America kept black men under control. And three-quarters of the way through his speech he described the extent of espionage in Paris. The audience was stunned. . . . He named names, dates, and places: Negroes who could "talk Communism" were being sent into the ghettos as well as into every colony of expatriate Americans. The agent provocateur had been introduced into the Black Belt for the first time.[48]

This *agent provocateur* appears in Wright's *Island of Hallucination,* a book which, although discussed by his biographer, Constance Webb, was apparently never published. The black spy is, however, well delineated by John A. Williams in his novel, *The Man Who Cried I Am* (see Chapter VIII).

Both these writers discovered that the black man's experience in America was excellent training for diplomacy abroad. The obsequious "darky" mask of slave tradition has continued to be a satisfactory subterfuge for the Afro-American. Behind that docile exterior, he has been able safely to filch out information and pick up the proper clues for survival in the white world. With certain refinements and embellishments, he has developed this ability far beyond the point of mere survival. As a confidence man abroad, he has joined the ranks of Melville's universal con man, with the final irony of black man leading black man into ultimate darkness.

NOTES

1. Richard Chase, *The American Novel and Its Tradition* (Garden City, New York, 1957), p. 7.
2. I am indebted to Charles R. Anderson for this phrase from *The Magic Circle of Walden* (New York, 1968), p. 39.
3. Walt Whitman, *Complete Poetry and Selected Prose*, ed. James E. Miller, Jr. (Boston, 1959), p. 68.
4. Leslie A. Fiedler, *No! in Thunder, Essays on Myth and Literature* (Boston, 1960), p. 67.
5. Henry David Thoreau, *The Writings of Henry David Thoreau*, Manuscript Edition (Boston, 1906) vol. I, p. 323-324.
6. Ibid., vol. II, p. 353.
7. Ibid., vol. II, p. 363.
8. Anderson, *Magic Circle*, p. 17.
9. J. A. Christie, *Thoreau as World Traveler* (New York, 1965), p. 267.
10. Thoreau, *The Writings*, vol. V, p. 246.
11. Ralph Ellison, *Invisible Man* (New York, 1952), pp. 438-439.
12. Thoreau, *The Writings*, vol. I, p. 130.
13. Richard Chase, *Walt Whitman Reconsidered* (New York, 1955), p. 16.
14. Ibid., p. 45.
15. Ibid., p. 51.
16. Ibid., p. 42.
17. Anderson, *Magic Circle*, p. 50.
18. Whitman, *Complete Poetry*, p. 108.
19. Chase, *Walt Whitman Reconsidered*, p. 104.
20. Herman Melville, *Moby-Dick or, The Whale*, ed. Charles Feidelson, Jr. (Indianapolis, 1964), p. 93. Further citations will be in the text.
21. Newton Arvin, *Herman Melville* (New York, 1950), p. 171.
22. Paul Brodtkorb, Jr., *Ishmael's White World, A Phenomenological Reading of "Moby Dick"* (New Haven, 1965), p. 21.
23. Ibid., p. 22.
24. Ibid., p. 123.
25. Ibid., p. 124
26. Ibid., p. 55
27. Constance Webb, *Richard Wright: A Biography* (New York, 1968), p. 363.
28. Robert E. Spiller et al., eds., *Literary History of the United States*, 3rd ed. (New York, 1963), p. 455.
29. Arvin, *Herman Melville*, p. 182.
30. R. W. Stallman, "Huck Finn Again," *College English* XVIII (May 1957): 425-426.
31. Leslie A. Fiedler, *Love and Death in the American Novel* (New York, 1966), p. 194.
32. James Fenimore Cooper, *The Complete Works*, Mohawk Edition (New York, 1912), V, p. 80-81. Further citations will be in the text.
33. Henry Nash Smith, Introduction, in James Fenimore Cooper, *The Prairie* (New

York, 1966), p. xvi.
34. Arvin, *Herman Melville*, p. 174.
35. Fiedler, *Love and Death*, p. 349.
36. Ibid., p. 349.
37. Leslie A. Fiedler, *The Return of the Vanishing American* (New York, 1968), p. 118.
38. Richard Chase (*The American Novel*, p. 51) makes this point about Natty Bumppo, but it also appears to be applicable to Ishmael Bush.
39. George Dekker, *James Fenimore Cooper, the Novelist* (London, 1967), p. 101.
40. Ibid., p. 59.
41. Chase, *The American Novel*, p. 51.
42. Herman Melville, *The Confidence-Man: His Masquerade*, ed. H. Bruce Franklin (New York, 1967), p. 14.
43. Richard Chase, *Herman Melville, A Critical Study* (New York, 1949), pp. 186-187.
44. Daniel G. Hoffman, *Form and Fable in American Fiction* (New York, 1961), p. 300.
45. Langston Hughes and Arna Bontemps, eds., *The Book of Negro Folklore* (New York, 1958), p. x.
46. Ralph Ellison, *Invisible Man* (New York, 1952), p. 376.
47. Ibid., p. 374.
48. Webb, *Richard Wright*, p. 377.

4. NATIVE AND EXPATRIATE SONS:
The Running Man in Wright and Baldwin

Richard Wright's autobiography links him to the tradition of the slave narrative. In *Black Boy*, the terror Wright felt when "escaping" from the South is amazingly similar to that experienced by the fugitive slave, and yet a hundred years had elapsed. Written and published after *Native Son*, Wright's autobiography had in some ways a greater impact than the novel on the American reading public, for the most part woefully ignorant of the Afro-American literary tradition. As Spiller points out:

While Wright's autobiography, *Black Boy* (1945) was more moderate in tone than his earlier novel, *Native Son*, it was probably even more merciless in its impact—for the horrors one could tolerate in the life of a fictional hero, one could hardly accept in the actual life of an ordinary citizen.[1]

Wright captures the tenacity of the fear-grip on the soul of the southern black. He is forced to steal, lie, shuffle, and "yessir" ignominiously in order to get to the road alive. For although he has been brutalized and discriminated against all of his life by southern whites, he experiences their typical reaction when he announces his intention to leave ("Southern whites hated the idea of Negroes leaving to live in places where the racial atmosphere was different"[2]). He is prepared, therefore, for the dialogue that takes place in the factory where he has been a menial:

"So you're going north, hunh?"
"Yes, sir. My family's taking me with 'em."
"The North's no good for your people, boy."
"I'll try to get along sir."

"Don't believe all the stories you hear about the North."
"No sir. I don't."
"You'll come back here where your friends are."
"Well, sir. I don't know."
"How're you going to act up there."
"Just like I act down here, sir."
"Would you speak to a white girl up there."
"Oh, no, sir. I'll act there just like I act here."
"Aw, no you won't. You'll change. Niggers change when they go north."
I wanted to tell him that I was going north precisely to change, but I did not. (Wright 1945, 224-225)

The plantation system, or at least its dregs, was deeply rooted in his psyche. He had been born on a plantation, and he assumed the traditional mask for the contemporary "massa." "This was the culture from which I sprang," he wrote. "This was the terror from which I fled" (Wright 1945, 225).

Few black writers are so closely akin in spirit to the rebellious, hate-ridden slave bursting his bonds, like Nat Turner and Gabriel Prosser, to avenge, or like Douglass, Grandy, and William Wells Brown, to escape to freedom. Douglass, himself a solitary child unable to relate to his numerous "brothers and sisters," was no more alienated from his family than Richard Wright was from his. If we are to accept the viewpoint of the "autobiographical persona" of *Black Boy*, Wright's familial environment was replete with violence and humiliation and devoid of either warmth or affection. Uncles, aunts, and grandparents apparently tried to adapt the boy to the ugly climate of Jim Crow. Yet in spite of this "education," Wright was unable to deal with the facts of southern life to which he was so brutally exposed. When he went to work for whites, he was ill-prepared for the tension he experienced in their company: "I was always to be conscious of it, brood over it, carry it in my heart, live with it, sleep with it, fight with it" (Wright 1945, 131).

Richard Wright could never be convinced that he was inferior, nor did he doubt his human worth. He developed the kind of fear and anxiety syndrome that many ex-slave narrators describe as a permanent part of their emotional existence. Many slaves were able to mask their hostility toward whites in order to survive, but Richard Wright was seething, angry, and rebellious by the time he was twelve. Fatherless, hungry, and ill-clothed, like the plantation child, he dreamed of escape to the "promised land," the North.

The overwhelming desire to rid himself of "non-identity," or a conventional identity assigned him by southern white society, was the impulse that set Richard Wright in motion. Ishmael, the wanderer-outcast, and

Leatherstocking, the critic of the settlement, abjured their social identity, as did Huck Finn. But the fugitive slave, the unmanned nameless victim of the slave system is surely the progenitor of Black Boy, Bigger Thomas, Big Boy, and Dave, the youthful runner of "Almos' a Man." All of Wright's "black boys" share the compulsion to be free of the restrictions of their environment, to find their identity as men. The choice for the fugitive slave was clear. The North was freedom; he ran toward a real destination—the land of freedmen and men born free. Not so for his heir in this century—history has intervened. For this reason "Almos' a Man" ends on a note of ambiguity: "Ahead the long rails were glinting in moonlight, stretching away, away to somewhere, somewhere where he could be a man . . . ."[3] Dave had never before left the South—he is a generation removed from Claude Brown—and his hope is based on ignorance of reality. But he is also at this point a fugitive from white justice, a young man whose greatest ambition is to acquire a gun, to him a symbol of manhood. He is forced to choose between flight or spending two years working to pay for the boss's mule which he has killed accidentally.[4] Flight has at least the aura of freedom; it also represents an act of choice, exercise of will, and a rejection of his lifelong role of "boy" in the South. The act of running, for Dave, is a step in the direction of identity even if that "somewhere where he could be a man" does not exist.

Black Boy also ends on an ambiguously hopeful note. Wright sounds like Ishmael pushing off from shore to probe the mysteries of the unknowable sea:

I was leaving the South to fling myself into the unknown, to meet other situations that would perhaps elicit from me other responses. And if I could meet enough of a different life, then, perhaps, gradually and slowly I might learn who I was and what I might be. (Wright 1945, 228)

The tone of the ending is not difficult to explain, because the book covers only those years leading up to Wright's acutal flight from the South, those years before he had been disabused of his notions about the promise of the North. Furthermore, Harper published only two-thirds of Wright's autobiography, omitting his experiences in Chicago and New York. "His editor explained that there was an acute paper shortage because of the war and that Harper was afraid it might run out of stock altogether."[5] (Webb, in her biography, quotes extensively from this final part in which hope quickly changes to despair.)

The promise of the North is a delusion, of course; it is the walled confines of Bigger Thomas's existence in Chicago. Restricted even more in choice than the southern "black boy" who still has his dream, Bigger, having already experienced the dead end of black life in the North, moves toward identity by living out the consequences of his actions: "Never had his will been so free as in this night and day of fear and murder and flight."[6]

Bigger's experience in the North can in some ways be considered the next stage in the life of the southern "black boy" whom Wright depicts in "Big Boy Leaves Home," the opening story in *Uncle Tom's Children* (1938). Big Boy, a reluctant Running Man, leaves home because it is the only way he can stay alive. The story opens in a deceptively idyllic southern setting with a group of adolescent boys whose simple truancy leads to death, lynching, and general disaster. When the boys emerge from swimming they are confronted by a white woman with a rifle who stands between them and their clothes. She screams for her husband who, without hesitation, shoots two of them. Big Boy wrestles with the white man for the gun and finally shoots him. Of the group, only Big Boy and Bobo are left alive. Big Boy returns home and tells his story, sending the black community into panic. Elder Sanders proposes that Big Boy hide in a deserted kiln until his son Will can come by in the morning and take him North to safety. While Big Boy is hiding he hears a mob, lynch-bound with Bobo, and he cannot avoid witnessing the act of barbarism committed against his friend.

In the morning Will arrives and Big Boy escapes, hidden beneath a trap door in the truck. Blyden Jackson emphasizes the contrast between the symbolic beginning of the story—a halcyon spring day, the boys open and free—and the final scene in which Big Boy is confined within the truck.[7] Big Boy's story does foreshadow Bigger's confined and constricted life in the Black Belt of Chicago; "Big Boy Leaves Home" also demonstrates forcefully the perversion of the ritual that most societies provide as a natural part of the passage from boy to man. One role is forbidden the black male in our society—that of man. The plantation slave remained a boy until he aged to "uncle." Rites of passage were denied young black males; in fact, castration was the most symbolic aspect of the lynching ritual, intended to serve as a horrifying, sadistic admonishment. Wright's protagonist in "Big Boy Leaves Home" is not much past puberty when he and his friends inadvertently break the sexual taboo by revealing their naked bodies to a white woman. What should be a comic youthful prank then becomes a tragic incident of violence and death. The lynching of his friend, which Big Boy is forced to watch from his hiding place, dramatically represents the way in which society punishes even an abortive attempt to achieve manhood.[8]

From the opening lines of the dozens, the verbal game of insult so much a part of the black folk experience ("Yo' mama don' wear no drawers . . .") to the fifth section describing the early morning chill and the loneliness and alienation of the young man hiding in the kiln, Wright captures the ambiance of the southern black experience. Big Boy's life is predictable. He and his friends talk about leaving the South in almost the same terms as the slaves did. In fact, Big Boy's journey North, like that of the runaway slave, is a flight from oppression and the threat of imminent death. Big Boy's role as runner is positive in that it is an escape to freedom. We know that in the twentieth century the North holds no promise for young or even older black men, but the negative aspects of running are not yet apparent in Wright's powerful novella, as they are in his first novel, *Native Son*.

In the opening section of *Native Son*, Bigger's mother characterizes his wasteful life as "running with that gang of yours," and admonishes him that "the gallows is at the end of the road you travelling" (Wright 1940, 8). Bigger's road is the narrow path of the petty thief, preying on the small storekeeper. He and his gang have been highly circumspect about their victims, preferring black storeowners because "they knew that white policemen never really searched diligently for Negroes who committed crimes against other Negroes" (Wright 1940, 12). But when he convinces the gang to broaden their activities, he is confronted with the need to carry out his own plan of attack against a white storeowner, and he is consumed by fear. Fear forces him to hide behind an aggressive exterior that obscures reality. Running *from* the self has only negative implications. It is an inversion of the pattern set by those nineteenth-century runners who were impelled toward new frontiers of awareness. An avoidance of knowledge, it is an escape that can only lead away from self-acceptance and toward self-hate. Instead of an expansion of the self, we see in Bigger a shrinking from perception and a consequent diminution of the self.

"Fear" is Wright's title for the first section of *Native Son*. Bigger's life has been one long internal flight from fear. He creates a mask behind which to hide from the pain of reality, and that mask of toughness is his protection against his family and the world. Toughness at times fails him, however, as when he realizes that he has taken on more than he can carry out in the robbery plan, for "it would be a symbolic challenge which they yearned to make, but were afraid to" (Wright 1940, 12). Bigger and Gus are the two most frightened gang members and Bigger depends on Gus's fear to obviate the necessity of acknowledging his own. Like Moby Dick for Ahab, Gus becomes for Bigger the object of all the hate and fear Bigger feels for the repressive white world—his objective correlative.

What happens to Bigger during this quandary in the pool hall foreshadows what will happen to him later when he is trapped in Mary's bedroom with the same fear and hate, between two women—one drunk and one blind—who represent the dreadful, unseeing yet immutable white world that controls him. This time, however, Bigger is confronted by one who sees *and* understands him. Gus is Bigger's other self, no longer under control, slipping into consciousness and alerting others and himself to reality. Bigger's reactions are in part visceral—his stomach burns, and "mixed images of violence" run "like sand through his mind." He has a terrible need to inflict pain, but he is thwarted as Gus agrees to the plan.

Bigger now must cope with the feelings from which he is always in psychic flight. Gus, the object of his hate and fear, is suddenly beyond reach, yet the tension generated by these violent emotional energies is still with him. A man determined to live outside his own feelings, Bigger is aware only that his emotional existence has a certain kind of ebb and flow and even this is nonvolitional; the "rhythms of his life" are "indifference and violence" (Wright 1940, 24-25). Bigger's indifference is what Charles Silberman calls "psychic withdrawal,"[9] a way of coping with failure and impotence. Bigger's running without motion is a response to powerlessness in the face of forces he cannot understand, and flight from blackness that confines him to an oppressive, walled-in world. Bigger hovers "unwanted between two worlds—between powerful America and his own stunted place in life," Wright says in his article on *Native Son*, "and I took upon myself the task of trying to make the reader feel this No Man's Land."[10]

Bigger's "No Man's Land" is also a psychological void, filled intermittently with fear, hate, desire, or dread. Violence for him is often an abortive attempt to conceal one or the other of these intense emotions. Bigger's life depends on his ability to avoid introspection, to run away from himself as he later runs from his pursuers:

He felt the same way toward everyone. As long as he could remember, he had never been responsible to anyone. The moment a situation became so that it exacted something of him, he rebelled. That was the way he lived; he passed his days trying to defeat or gratify powerful impulses in a world be feared. (Wright 1940, 36)

These powerful and inexplicable impulses finally lead him to murder.

In *Native Son*, running becomes a criminal activity. It differs from the criminal activity of the confidence man, however, mainly because instead of arising from a premeditated plan of illegal action, it is a result of that action, a compulsive attempt to escape the law:

He had to save himself. But it was familiar, this running away. All his life he had been knowing that sooner or later something like this would come to him. And now, here it was. He had always felt outside of this white world, and now it was true. (Wright 1940, 87-88)

Following the inexorable law of his deterministic existence, Bigger is both victim and murderer; he is catapulted into criminal action by the circumstances of his life, not by direct, self-interested choice. Being a destroyer gives Bigger an identity: "What his knife and gun once meant to him, his knowledge of having secretly murdered Mary now meant" (Wright 1940, 127).

Mary's death is accidental, but it originates in the abortive design of Bigger's life, his enforced proximity to whites with whom he (and they with him) cannot deal, and their obtuseness. Max, the lawyer who takes the hopeless case, emphasizes Bigger's instinctive, unthinking reaction to his situation, the fact that "he has murdered many times but there are no corpses" (Wright 1940, 335). How closely this resembles the instincts of the ex-slave who smoldered with hate and lashed out in circumstances where he apparently had nothing to gain and his life to lose.

There are other similarities to the slave narrative in *Native Son*. "Flight," the longest section of the book (it is also in the general three-section pattern), recalls the suspenseful flight of the slave narrator. In his compulsion to be free, Bigger shares the positive impulse toward survival that characterized the runaway slave. Bigger's terror is much like that of the fugitive slave with the armed servants of the law and the master at his back, his blackness a visible indication of the geographic boundary to which he was restricted. Bigger is bound by the Black Belt of Chicago, his movements also restricted by his color, and when he is tracked down and captured in the bitter, surely symbolic snow, he is ringed by white faces of the law.

We know at the end that Bigger's attempt to merge with others and "be a part of this world, to lose himself in it so he could find himself, to be allowed to live like others, even though he was black" (Wright 1940, 204), is a failure. While Mary's death leads him to his first, inchoate feelings of being alive, it also leads inevitably to his own death.

Other running men have failed. Gatsby's flight (from the past), tinctured with criminal activity, is in essence a romantic flight *back* into the past of which Daisy is a part. His attempt to don an identity acceptable to her leads to failure of the dream and, eventually, his death. Gatsby's dream is shared in part by other runners of the twenties, like Nick Carraway (whose flight to the East fails because he is "subtly unadaptable to Eastern life"[11]): a belief in the "orgiastic future" that receded before them but toward which they continued to run—"So we beat on, boats against the current, borne back ceaselessly into the past" (Fitzgerald 1925, 218). Beatific runners of the fifties also failed: Dean Moriarty's restless flight back and forth across the continent is a six thousand mile treadmill with no beginning and no end. But Bigger Thomas's experience as a black man in America separates him from these white running men of the present as it does from those of the past. All make deliberate decisions to run; none is restricted by skin color. While the Afro-American's race is almost always visible, his humanity is not. At the beginning of *Native Son* Bigger feels that he is outside the white world ("Half the time I feel like I'm on the outside of the world peeping in through a knot-hole in the fence"), and for him this state is as ceaseless and unchanging as the tides. "At the end of *Native Son*," according to Blyden Jackson, "the world of Bigger Thomas does not differ from that he has always known. . . . Bigger has made an effort to redefine his relationship with this world." Yet "we know that he has not succeeded in meaningful terms."[12] Bigger's compulsion to run for his life *back* to the confines of the Black Belt, surely not the road to freedom, confirms how far outside the white world he actually is. Eminently clear, however, is the truth of Wright's conception: Bigger's world, in spite of its violent motion, is one of negative stasis, and Bigger's running is finally and inescapably a return to the beginning.

Richard Wright was obsessed with the psychological dislocation, the outside-ness of the black man in America, not just his physical isolation:

The fact of separation from the culture of his native land has sunk into the Negro's heart. The Negro loves his land, but that land rejects him. He is always apart. He is, God help him, always alone.[13]

Wright transformed this obsession into a novel, *The Outsider* (1953). Far more self-conscious and articulate an outsider than Bigger Thomas is Cross Damon, the protagonist, who, having sloughed off his old identity after an accident in which he is presumed to have died, is in a sense free to become his own conception. But existential freedom is accompanied by Dread, the title of Book I, and in its wake, terror:

Now, depending only upon his lonely will, he saw that to map out his life entirely upon his own assumptions was a task that terrified him just to think of it, for he knew that he first had to know what he thought life was, had to know consciously all the multitude of assumptions which other men took for granted. . . .[14]

Like most running men, Cross flees from home and family; however, he is inundated by complex and overwhelming responsibilities for a kind of multi-family, deployed in different homes: an estranged wife and three children, a pregnant girlfriend, and an aging, poor, hyper-religious mother. By comparison, the life of the nineteenth-century Running Man was an ecstasy of freedom! A subway accident suddenly awakens Cross to the possibility of escape from his intolerable obligations and the intimidating conditions of his old life.

Freedom, however, is not so easily attainable, and Cross finds that the act of running becomes for him a criminal activity:

In a way he was a criminal, not so much because of what he was doing, but because of what he was feeling. It was for much more than merely criminal reasons that he was fleeing to escape his identity, his old hateful consciousness. There was a kind of innocence that made him want to shape for himself the kind of life he felt he wanted, but he knew that that innocence was deeply forbidden. (Wright 1953, 78)

This deeply forbidden innocence is undoubtedly that of the first man and Cross is in some ways a contemporary Adam with godlike pretensions, a demonic man hurling himself against all the coldness, the ugliness, and the despair of modern existence. Doomed to failure, he is destined to try again and again with all the passion for life that Ihab Hassan ascribes to the modern "hero," whose awareness and unquenchable passion he calls "radical innocence."[15]

Cross's flight is a persistent attempt to order his own universe amid the chaos of society by creating an identity with which he can live. His various names (and protean guises) seem to reflect the stages through which he passes: Webb, when he is still trapped in Chicago; Jordan, when he is free of his past and escapes to New York; and Lane, his final road, which is narrow indeed. Running ceases to be a metaphor for freedom when Cross takes upon himself the judgment and death of others. It becomes a completely negative criminal activity when it isolates him from human emotions and allows him to kill "like flies to wanton boys." What began as an escape to freedom in order to redefine his life in his own terms, so that he could relate to others who "had thought their way through the many veils of illusion" (Wright 1953, 25), becomes instead a flight without direction. It leaves him more appallingly alone than he was before he took to the road:

But where could he run to? And what was he running from? He knew that in any hiding place, under whatever guise he chose to conceal himself, he would be alone with himself to meditate in dismay the ungovernable compulsiveness of himself and the loss of his sense of direction in life. (Wright 1953, 303)

What was for Thoreau a positive journey, a flight into the self for discovery and perfection, is for Cross Damon a recessive step into a self with shrinking resources. Wright's fictional runner is finally unable to govern his emotions or to control his ceaseless activity. A century of philosophic and historic distance separates the transcendental from the existential runner.

The most significant aspect of *The Outsider* for our purposes is Wright's enunciation, through Ely Houston, of the "double vision" he attributes to the black man:

"Negroes, as they enter our culture, are going to inherit the problems we have, but with a difference. They are outsiders and they are going to *know* that they have these problems. They are going to be self-conscious; they are going to be gifted with a double vision, for, being Negroes, they are going to be both *inside* and *outside* of our culture at the same time. Every emotional and cultural convulsion that ever shook the heart and soul of Western man will shake them. Negroes will develop unique and specially defined psychological types. . . . They will not only be Americans or Negroes; they will be centers of *knowing.* . . ." (Wright 1953, 119)

This quality of vision we have already seen in the Running Man who, by virtue of always being an outsider, is psychologically and (often) physically located in a No Man's Land, from which he is able to see in more than one direction. For this reason, a certain critical stance is associated with virtually all of the running men discussed thus far: the old Trapper and Ishmael Bush as the dual consciousness of Cooper confronted with the inexorable movement of civilization; Huck and Jim as Twain's sense of integrity in opposition to society's "moral sense"; Thoreau as the persistent seeker after perfection in a flawed society; and the fugitive slave as the symbol of freedom juxtaposed against social cynicism.

Most of Wright's protagonists, including himself as "Black Boy," are running men in the tradition we have been considering, even though their running is a more negative act. Wright's contribution to the Running Man metaphor is his conception of the black man as a "center of knowing," a Running Man with the added dimension of "dreadful objectivity":

"Now, imagine a man inclined to think, to probe, to ask questions. Why he'd be in a wonderful position to do so, would he not, if he were black and lived in America? A dreadful objectivity would be forced upon him." (Wright 1953, 119)

This self-conscious observer *is* the Running Man in contemporary Afro-American literature, the metaphorical figure with whom Ellison, Baldwin, Brown, Kelley, Baraka, Davis, *et al.*, deal. He differs from the black Running Man of the nineteenth century in that the fugitive slave was not both outside and inside our culture at the same time. Rather than knowing less because he has not experienced centuries of western acculturation, the black man, Wright insists, sees more deeply and will know more because he has been forced into the position of dreadful objectivity: "Some men are so placed in life by accident of race or birth or chance that what they see is terrifying" (Wright 1953, 123). The very fact of his existence in America has bestowed this "gift" of double vision upon the black man and placed him in a unique position to be a critical, if not dispassionate, observer.

The later black runner, with his special vision and heightened consciousness, also differs from the running men of the nineteenth century in that his running is far more complex. The outsider, for example, is a victim of the twentieth-century ethos which has instilled in him anonymity, facelessness and, paradoxically, dependence. Unlike the westerner, Melville's Ishmael, and especially Thoreau, he cannot function alone. Always an outsider of the mind, Cross Damon is—by virtue of the subway accident—able to choose outsideness as a way of life with the opportunity to build an identity, a self apart from the identity forced upon him by society. But he fails. Instead of delighting in being alone to perfect his self, he suffers from a terrifying alienation and his self disintegrates. He needs others who are also outsiders by choice, like Ely Houston, and his dying admonishment to Houston reflects this painful perception: Don't try it alone, it's horrible! Apparently the twentieth century has deprived man of his self-reliance, his independence, his individuality. Cross Damon is without that solid layer of confident self-reliance that characterized the nineteenth-century Running Man, and therefore he never apprehends the higher law of conscience without which he cannot control his impulses. Yet, ironically, Cross is also a kind of promethean demon who aspires more to the role of God than to the perfectibility of man. In an attempt to become supra-human, he finally steps outside the bounds of human sensibility.

Wright placed himself permanently outside America when he became, like the Crafts and other ex-slaves a century earlier, one of the most famous American expatriates in Europe after World War II. For the rest of his life he remained a fugitive from America, the prototype of the black Running Man abroad. His last published novel, *The Long Dream* (1958), ends with Fishbelly escaping North, after his father is murdered by the police, and taking a plane to Paris. Constance Webb calls the book a second "autobiography" and notes Wright's concern about having once more written of a Running Man:

Once again, he had allowed his hero to solve a problem by running away. What he intended, and hoped the public would see, was that it was symbolic of those who first settled America. The white settlers had also been running away from problems which they had been helpless to solve in the environments in which they had lived in Europe. And the early Americans actually had solved their problems by running and creating a new life on a new continent. In *Long Dream* the geography is reversed but the problem is the same. Fish seeks the possibility of a new life in Paris, one which he cannot possibly find in Mississippi. Fish is a descendant of men who had not come to America voluntarily but were brought forcibly and compelled to give up their freedom for slavery.[16]

Nothing could more effectively relate Richard Wright to the tradition of the Running Man, both black and white.

Fishbelly's life in Paris, *Island of Hallucination*, was never published, but a similarity surely not accidental—exists between the real Richard Wright abroad and the fictional Harry Ames in John A. Williams's novel. *The Man Who Cried I Am*, discussed in detail in Chapter VIII, deals with the subterranean role of a number of black expatriates of the kind that Fishbelly, Wright's persona, encounters. Williams develops what Wright apparently intended in *Hallucination*, the character of the black espionage agent shaped to the reality of the Cold War, an "ideal" role for the uprooted black Running Man.

James Baldwin's own impulse to run, like Richard Wright's, was born of a conviction that he could not function completely as an artist and a man in white America:

I left America because I doubted my ability to survive the fury of the color problem here. (Sometimes I still do.) I wanted to prevent myself from becoming *merely* a Negro; or, even, merely a Negro writer. I wanted to find out in what way the *specialness* of my experience could be made to connect me with other people instead of dividing me from them.[17]

Wright's expatriation was permanent, Baldwin's of only ten years' duration. Both, however, used the theme of expatriation in their writing. We have already mentioned Wright's Running Man as expatriate; Baldwin's Running Man (David of *Giovanni's Room*), however, is entirely different from Wright's Fishbelly. He is a blond Anglo-Saxon whose "ancestors conquered a continent, pushing across death-laden plains, until they came to an ocean which faced away from Europe into a darker past."[18] At the outset, Baldwin relates David to those early American pioneers of the westward movement, the Running Man of the nineteenth century, at the same time suggesting the darker aspects of the running theme. That movement's twentieth-century counterpart is the restless flight *East*, back to New York, back to Europe, and David follows the pattern, going from San Francisco to New York and Paris.

There is something fantastic in the spectacle I now present to myself of having run so far, so hard, across the ocean even, only to find myself brought up short once more before the bulldog in my own backyard—the yard, in the meantime, having grown smaller and the bulldog bigger. (Baldwin 1956, 7)

The Running Man of the mid-twentieth century recognizes, in his lucid moments, that there is no place to run to, no place where he can escape "the bulldog in his own backyard." The animal here grown to full proportions is David's sexual inversion, which at this point he is forced to recognize as a permanent part of his past as well as his present. As a younger man he attempted to keep this knowledge from himself and from others, especially his father, whom he had come to despise. However, during the period of introspection which introduces the novel, David attempts, like Ellison's nameless hero, to look back over his life in order to extract from it some meaning for his present anguish. Most of his life has been a literal and actual flight from himself, for flight from one's country is essentially flight from one's own past. However, as Baldwin has often said, the past must be absorbed, not obliterated, in order for one to live successfully in the present.

David's running then, is essentially negative, devoid of higher values and without the real sense of protest against society that can be seen so often in the runners of the past. It resembles, however, the flight from home and family we have already seen in most running men, in particular Ishmael, Huck, and Natty Bumppo. A resemblance can also be seen to their "homoerotic" relationships: Ishmael and Queequeg, Huck and Jim, Natty and Chingachgook. The basically innocent, unexplored relationships between men in these novels is explored in depth by Baldwin and is central to his theme of a young man's search for identity. The Running Man metaphor is given a deliberate psychological ambiguity, for running is here an abortive attempt at self-delusion. Flight from home and family is occasioned by the failure of father and son to communicate and the confusion of the man's role in a distorted family group where a dead wife presides from the grave. The young man's alienation becomes complete when he discovers his homosexual feelings and is terrified of their implications. From that time on, he plays an intricate game of self-deception.

Without the security of family ties, David manages for a while to live alone with his fears by denying their existence, by not looking at himself, by "remaining, in effect, in constant motion" (Baldwin 1956, 3); finally, by running from America. Later, in looking back over his disastrous relationships with Giovanni and Hella, he says:

I think now that if I had any intimation that the self I was going to find would turn out to be only the same self from which I had spent so much time in flight, I would have stayed at home. But, again, I think I knew, at the very bottom of my heart, exactly what I was doing when I took the boat for France." (Baldwin 1956, 31)

At the time of his retrospective venture into insight, David is mired in guilt for having destroyed his relationship with his fiancée, Hella, by his liaison with Giovanni, who is about to be executed for murder. David's real guilt, as Baldwin projects it, is not his homosexual relationship with Giovanni, but his inability to commit himself to any relationship, his constitutional inability to love. To Baldwin, this malfunction of the psyche is American in origin, a national infirmity. Hella too has difficulty committing herself to marriage, but her hesitation is a minor peccadillo compared to David's cowardice in allowing her to find out for herself that he and Giovanni have been lovers.

Giovanni, on the other hand, is a stereotypical Italian—warm, exuberant, loyal, unafraid of committing himself to love but afraid of death. He is also an expatriate, a runner like David and Hella, but he has run from death, not life. Ironically, death is what he finds in Paris after David's desertion, having finally run the gamut of self-degradation in the underworld of the aging homosexuals, Giullaume and Jacques.

Giovanni's room is the symbolic cul-de-sac of homosexuality and David cannot yet accept its inevitability: "'The Americans always fly. They are not serious,' says Guillaume" (Baldwin 1956, 226). David's sense of survival is stronger than his sense of loyalty and his desire for love. His real motivation, however, is fear. He knows that if he does not escape Giovanni's room, he will have to face the reality of what he is—that identity from which he has run so far and for so long. David leaves Giovanni as abruptly as he left Joey, the boy with whom he had his first sexual encounter many years before. "My flight may indeed have begun that summer—which does not tell me where to find the germ of the dilemma which resolved itself, that summer, into flight" (Baldwin 1956, 14). The dilemma he never resolves is implicit in his recurrent childhood nightmare about his dead mother:

I scarcely remember her at all, yet she figured in my nightmares, blind with worms, her hair as dry as metal and brittle as a twig, straining to press me against her body; that body so putrescent, so sickening soft, that it opened, as I clawed and cried, into a breach so enormous as to swallow me alive (Baldwin 1956, 15)

Women and death are ineluctably linked in a kind of macabre plot to seduce men into the soft grave of their bodies. With such unrelieved repressions, David's manhood is always at stake, no matter how far he runs.

In his mind David lives Giovanni's journey to the guillotine; that journey precipitates his own unalterable course. Like Ishmael, David is destined to wander; one of the few survivors of the aberrant quest in Paris, he too ends a misanthrope. Freedom was the great quest of the early Running Man, particularly the fugitive slave, but the contradiction facing the expatriated runner is that he is unsure of himself and even suffers from emotional dislocation once he has achieved the freedom he so earnestly sought. "Nothing is more unbearable, once one has it, " David thinks, "than freedom." Baldwin describes this strange ambivalence in his introduction to *Nobody Knows My Name,* where he relates it to the black expatriate's feelings once he is free of America's color barrier:

Nothing is more desirable than to be released from an affliction, but nothing is more frightening than to be divested of a crutch. It turned out that the question of who I was was not solved because I had removed myself from the social forces which menaced me—anyway, these forces had become interior, and I had dragged them across the ocean with me. The question of who I was had at last become a personal question, and the answer was to be found in me.[19]

David's search for identity is confounded by his even stronger compulsion to escape the knowledge he harbors in his soul. The answer that he seeks is in himself, as Baldwin deduced about his own identity.

Although we cannot safely generalize from the one work in which the expatriate runner figures prominently, it is clear from *Giovanni's Room* that Baldwin, like other black writers of his generation, is creatively conversant with the Running Man metaphor.[20] His runner is expatriate, American, homosexual, and unconvincingly white. The ambiguity of his flight is based on his creator's ambivalence, which exists on three levels: national, sexual, and racial. For Baldwin, to be an American (white) is to be unable to love, a sickness of the psyche that inevitably dehumanizes. If one is unable to commit oneself to a love relationship, regardless of the sexual context, he loses his identity as a member of the human community, This is the plight of the protagonist in *Giovanni's Room*, who is unable to realize the extent of his malady. Trapped as he is by the problem of sexual morality, David thinks that homosexual love will rob him of his masculinity. Thus, instead of entering completely into the relationship with Giovanni, as Jacques advises him, he turns and runs. He violates the trust of both Giovanni and Hella and thus becomes an isolate from the human community. His flight, then, is essentially negative because it is a fruitless attempt to escape his real self, the acceptance of which is in fact the only way he can become a man.

If one runs from America as David does (and as Baldwin did), one almost of necessity loses one's identity as an American—which is to say as anything—for the expatriate lives in a limbo of nonbeing. David resents being called an American because it seems to make him nothing more than that, "whatever that was"; and he resents being called not American because it seems to make him nothing. Compare David's fictional ambivalence with Baldwin's description of the black expatriate's attitude in "Encounter on the Seine":

He finds himself involved, in another language, in the same old battle: the battle for his own identity. To accept the reality of his being an American becomes a matter involving his integrity and his greatest hopes, for only by accepting this reality can he hope to make articulate to himself or to others the uniqueness of his experience, and to set free the spirit so long anonymous and caged.[21]

The plight of the black expatriate has another painful dimension: he cannot relate to his fellow (white) Americans, who usually shun him; or to his fellow (black) Americans, who in general shun him and are shunned by him; or to the African, who carries his identity with him no matter where he is; or to the white European, who often does not treat him as an American out of an excess of friendliness, thereby depriving him of any identity whatsoever. Indeed, the "American Negro in Paris is very nearly the invisible man."[22] We have here the Running Man metaphor that points both to Wright and to Ellison, the "nonidentity" of the outsider and the Invisible Man.

The conclusion from Baldwin's logic is that the homosexual has more in common with the black American, especially the black expatriate, than he has with other white Americans, at home or abroad. The experience of the black expatriate in Europe is not too far removed from that of the homosexual, wherever he is, when he tries to escape what he is. He has in a real sense been psychologically bruised by a society that treats both blacks and homosexuals as something less than human. The only way these outsiders can avoid being permanently crippled is to face the reality of who they are. They must establish themselves in relation to the past; that way lies self-acceptance, identity, visibility.

Both Wright and Baldwin deal essentially with an inversion of the Running Man pattern. The nineteenth-century runner was positively oriented toward a goal which, if not always attainable, was in the realm of the possible. Even the runaway slave qualitatively changed his life when he fled North. The "escape" of Black Boy and Wright's protagonists Big Boy and Dave, however, is equivocal, for we know that the North was not the "promised land" for black men. Some, like Fishbelly, Wright himself, and Baldwin for a time, kept running as expatriates. Others, like Bigger Thomas and Cross Damon, took the escape route to criminality. The frustrations of life in the unyielding Black Belt have bred a personality in whom many of the normal human emotions are stillborn or slowly die of strangulation. Such individuals are in fact often out of touch with themselves. Bigger's deliberate flight from self-knowledge is an inversion of Whitman's and Thoreau's inward journey and exploration of the self. Baldwin's protagonist in *Giovanni's Room* responds similarly to self-knowledge. David is an expatriate of the self. His flight has only negative connotations because he continually runs *from* but never *to* anything: from America, his father, Giovanni, Hella, and ultimately from himself. The negative variant of the running pattern does, however, reveal some significant insights into the nature of the black experience in America.

NOTES

1. Robert E. Spiller et al., eds., *Literary History of the United States*, 3rd ed. (New York, 1963), p. 1315.

2. Richard Wright, *Black Boy* (New York, 1945), p. 223. Further citations will be in the text.

3. Richard Wright, "Almos' a Man" in *Anthology of American Negro Literature*, ed. Sylvestre C. Watkins (New York, 1966), p. 15.

4. The Moss Brothers, Big Mat, Melody, and Chinatown, also take to the road under circumstances surrounding the death of a mule. See William Attaway's novel, *Blood on the Forge*, originally published in 1941, one year after *Native Son*.

5. Constance Webb, *Richard Wright: A Biography* (New York, 1968), p. 203.

6. Richard Wright, *Native Son* (New York, 1940), p. 203. Further citations will be in the text.

7. Blyden Jackson in a lecture, "Contemporary Black American Fiction," given at Indiana University, November 6, 1968.

8. See Phyllis R. Klotman, "The White Bitch Archetype in Contemporary Black Fiction," *The Bulletin of the Midwest Modern Language Association* (Spring 1973): 101.

9. Charles Silberman, *Crisis in Black and White* (New York, 1964), p. 119.

10. Richard Wright, *How "Bigger" Was Born* (New York, 1940), p. xxxvii.

11. F. Scott Fitzgerald, *The Great Gatsby* (New York, 1925), p. 212. Further citations will be in the text.

12. Blyden Jackson, "The Negro's Image of His Universe as Reflected in His Fiction," *Images of the Negro in America*, ed. Darwin T. Turner and Jean M. Bright (Boston, 1966), p. 89.

13. Quoted by J. Saunders Redding, "Alien Land of Richard Wright," *Soon, One Morning* (New York, 1966), p. 52.

14. Richard Wright, *The Outsider* (New York, 1953), p. 83. Further citations will be in the text.

15. Ihab Hassan, *Radical Innocence* (Princeton, New Jersey, 1961), p. 6.

16. Webb, *Richard Wright*, p. 362.

17. James Baldwin, *Nobody Knows My Name* (New York, 1961), p. 3.

18. James Baldwin, *Giovanni's Room* (New York, 1956), p. 3. Further citations will be in the text.
19. James Baldwin, *Nobody Knows My Name*, p. xii.
20. It might be argued that all of Baldwin's protagonists are running men, particularly Rufus Scott in *Another Country* but none has quite the same syndrome as David. Eric and Yves (also in *Another Country*) could be thought of as David and Giovanni with hope; Leo Proudhammer, Barbara King, and Black Christopher (*Tell Me How Long The Train's Been Gone*) could be a David-Hella-Giovanni trio in delicate balance. Neither Eric nor Leo, however, suffers from David's expatriation affliction, nor does either find himself in continual flight from "the bulldog in his backyard." What is even more important, both are able to commit themselves in love. Rufus, on the other hand, finds his commitment destructive to others, especially Leona, as well as to himself. Although his brief, agonized life ends in suicide, his influence subtly pervades the novel.
21. James Baldwin, *Notes of a Native Son* (Boston, 1955), p. 121.
22. Baldwin, *Notes*, p. 118.

5. ELLISON:
"Keep That Nigger-Boy Running"

Ralph Ellison's *Invisible Man* is the culmination of the Running Man metaphor, the electric "umbilical cord" connecting the running men of the past with those of the present. In no other single work is the metaphor as central to the meaning and significance of the artist's overall conception; in no other work is the ambiguity so consistently sustained. Indeed, running gives shape and unity to the novel. While the prologue and epilogue are static—in both sections the protagonist is immobilized, even though the epilogue intimates a change—the central section is a series of spasmodic movements in flight.

Unlike the slave, who exercised volition in his desire and decision to escape, Ellison's protagonist is essentially a runner by coercion, precipitated into flight by some unwitting but irrevocable blunder. His *faux pas*, though seemingly self-initiated, are for the most part governed by those all-but-invisible puppet strings, manipulated by the forces of power in whatever form they manifest themselves: the southern white power structure, the black college, the factory system, industrial unionism, the Brotherhood. Running, then, as revealed in the dream quotation, is a negative uncontrolled response to a metaphoric cattle prod used by others to shock the Invisible Man into random, indiscriminate movement, leaving him impotent, without control over himself or his environment (symbolized specifically in the "hospital" scene, which is ambiguously rebirth *and* the partial death of emasculation). The protagonist never controls his environment—that great Hemingway ideal—until he stops running *physically* and is alone, reflective, visible at least to himself.

From the vantage point of his underground isolation, the narrator in the prologue begins to look back and to reevaluate his experiences, to expose his life retrospectively to the reader and to himself. The technique, in the tradition of Wright's underground man (cf. "The Man Who Lived Underground")[1] as well as Dostoevsky's, is redolent with that irony that seems to have flowed almost unconsciously from the pens of ex-slave narrators. His underground retreat is like another country, and the Invisible Man becomes a kind of expatriate in the subterranean "country" that is his temporary home. Richard Kostelanetz also calls attention to this aspect of the narrator's nonparticipation:

Whereas Rinehart exploited absurdity for personal gain, the narrator as underground man accepts, as an expatriate, the condition through his own non-participation.[2]

"Expatriation" separates the nameless narrator in time and space from the mayhem of his unilluminated existence aboveground: "Before that I lived in darkness into which I was chased, but now I see."[3] The Invisible Man's testimony makes clear that running had been involuntarily induced; he is not yet aware of his own internal escape mechanism. Actually, "the forces from without and internal dissension from within reduce invisible man to the state of flight"[4] and propel him into frustration (darkness), not freedom. Through the inadvertent courtesy of Monopolated Light and Power, however, 1,369 light bulbs have taken the shape of a klieg-light sun, eliminating time and making the darkness of his hibernation forever light, his invisibility visible. "Light confirms my reality, gives birth to my form" (Ellison 1952, 5). Now he can in reality, and for the first time, see his past as did the expatriate Baldwin, who, from the vantage point of his Swiss retreat, "began to try to recreate the life that [he] had first known as a child and from which [he] had spent so many years in flight."[5] Nonparticipation is not, then, a negative activity for the expatriated narrator. Rather, it is a time for self-reflective breath-catching, a time to throw the light of humor, horror, and history into the shadows before he again moves into action.

The major part of the book is an account of the narrator's life: the first half, an escape from various unsatisfactory social identities, leading to the climactic death-and-rebirth section; the second half, the quest for a new identity, and in common with Harry Angstrom and Holden Caulfield, the search for an "environment in which he can perform at his best," the result "a painful contemporary odyssey."[6] The epilogue rounds the work to a finish with an indication of renewed activity: "Without the possibility of action, all knowledge comes to one labeled 'file and forget,' and I can neither file nor forget" (Ellison 1952, 437). True, there is no final resolution; the Running Man metaphor remains ambiguous, because running for Ellison as for Thoreau is striving, and therefore a function of life. The narrator, like Thoreau, absents himself from society for a time, although not initially by choice—the black experience in America has a way of eliminating free will. *His* Walden is not a pond but a hole; he has not walked out to it of his own volition, but fallen *into* it while attempting to escape with his life.

I felt myself plunge down, down; a long drop that ended upon a load of coal that sent up a cloud of dust, and I lay in the black dark upon the black coal no longer running, hiding or concerned. (Ellison 1952, 427)

His flight is unwittingly into hibernation, but once there he pursues self-knowledge in the airless dark, in the company of nature's emboweled offering, with a moral intensity equal to that of the nineteenth-century seeker in the pure and open air. Running as ratiocination, then, becomes a positive pursuit, not a compulsive escape, and Running Man has become "thinker Tinker."

Once "clubbed into his cellar" and losing the world, the Invisible Man learns the difficulty of looking into one's self:

When one is invisible he finds such problems as good and evil, honesty and dishonesty, of such shifting shapes that he confuses one with the other, depending upon who happens to be looking through him at the time. Well, now I've been trying to look through myself, and there's a risk in it. (Ellison 1952, 432)

At risk may be more than being hated when trying to be honest, or liked when dishonestly affirming someone else's mistaken beliefs; the risk may be the trauma when one is confronted, as Cross Damon was, with the specter of a formless self and the incumbent responsibility, albeit opportunity, to shape one's own identity. We have already examined the protean nature of the Running Man, his empathy for other outsiders (Cross Damon—Ely Houston, Ishmael—Ahab) and his capacity to identify with the hunted and harried (Natty Bumppo and the red Running Man, Huck and Jim). What we see most clearly in Ellison's protagonist is this protean quality, which differs in degree from Wright's outsider and in kind from Cooper's westerner. In the manner of Indian tradition, Cooper assigns different epithets to his protagonist commensurate with his changing identity in each novel. Natty Bumppo is Deerslayer, Hawkeye, Leatherstocking, the old Trapper; all of these names *reflect* his various accomplishments. Yet he is still Natty Bumppo. Wright's Running Man assumes various aliases to *conceal* his identity (in order to protect himself from the consequences of criminal activity) and eventually loses touch with himself. The protean quality of Ellison's protagonist is symbolized by the namelessness of the character and is artistically related to the Running Man metaphor, for each time he takes flight his identity is subtly altered or drastically changed. As one critic has pointed out, "If you are no one, you are at the same time potentially everyone."[7]

To Ellison, Proteus is both America and "the inheritance of illusion through which all men must fight to achieve reality."[8] The writer must

challenge the apparent forms of reality—that is, the fixed manners and values of the few, and . . . struggle with it until it reveals its mad, vari-implicated chaos, its false faces, and on until it surrenders its insight, its truth. (Ellison 1952, 106)

Isn't this also the struggle of the nameless narrator in *Invisible Man*? The forms of reality with which he struggles stubbornly refuse to reveal their truth, so that he himself takes up the masks, the false faces, that reveal only chaos. Ironically, he is both Proteus, struggling and turning into diverse shapes, and the grandson of Proteus, holding and pressing the past so that he can achieve reality in the present.

The first identity the narrator assumes is conventional for a bright southern Negro boy: he imagines himself another Booker T. Washington. That ill-fitting guise doesn't alter drastically even when he makes his first portentous blunder, a Freudian slip of the tongue changing social "responsibility" into social "equality." Only the dream, ineluctably linked to the stolid black peasantry of his past—symbolized by his grandfather—mocks his false face and sets him mentally on the road. The white-man's-black-man identity fades into unreality when his next irrevocable error threatens the myth so carefully nurtured by the southern black educator. Dr. Bledsoe makes a reality of the nightmarish dream. Because the young idealist hasn't learned "to act the nigger," Bledsoe propels him onto the road North, ostensibly because "the race needs good, smart disillusioned fighters" (Ellison 1952, 112), but actually because his own position of power depends upon the docility and blindness, or covert compliance, of the young.

Bewildered by his loss of identity—"here within this quiet greenness I possessed the only identity I had ever known, and I was losing it" (Ellison 1952, 77)—the protagonist runs North with "letters of recommendation" from Bledsoe, honorably unopened in his treasured briefcase, a gift from the good white citizens in the distant past of his white-man's black-man identity. But the letters, one for each day in the week, open no doors, and he begins to feel that he is playing a part in some scheme he cannot understand. No matter how he wrings his mind, the scheme will not reveal its truth. What is his role, his new identity? Who assigns the roles—northern whites or southern black educators? He doesn't find the answers to all of these questions but he desperately tries to prove his "identity" to the disenchanted son of his seventh and last hope. This liberal son of a northern industrialist lives in his own masquerade world and offers the confused narrator a more sophisticated role in his version of an old classic: Huck and Jim at the Club Calamus. But the young narrator doesn't understand the double entendre and keeps insisting that he has another identity. "'Identity!' 'Huckleberry' Emerson cries, 'My God! Who has any identity any more anyway?'" (Ellison 1952, 142). Then he reveals the information that impels the protagonist again to flight."'I beg of you, sir,' Bledsoe says in his letter to Emerson the father, 'to help him continue in the direction of that promise which, like the horizon, recedes ever brightly and distantly beyond the hopeful traveler'" (Ellison 1952, 145). Nowhere is there a more sardonic treatment of the Emersonian style of northern intellectual, the man who deals in instant self-reliance; obviously Ralph Waldo Ellison has a special antipathy for the type.

As hopeless traveler and black pariah, the protagonist blunders into the role of union scab at Liberty Paints, artfully conceived as a microcosm of both American society and the industrial complex. A neophyte laborer, he commits an unpardonable error in paint mixing by exceeding the ten black drops that assure pure American whitewash. This blunder reveals the invisible contributions of black people to America (as did his off-campus error of exposing atavistic Trueblood of the black past to the delicate white sensibility), and projects him into an abortive conflict with Brockway, who represents the black foundation on which society and industry rest. The importance of outside pressure (the gauges) is forgotten as the two men lock in a black-against-black struggle (comparable to "battle royal") while the factory explodes, at least in the protagonist's mind. "'I seemed to run swiftly up an incline and shot forward with sudden acceleration into a wet blast of black emptiness that was somehow a bath of whiteness" (Ellison 1952, 175). He is thus projected, like human fallout, into the climactic hospital scene, which symbolizes both death and rebirth. Immaculately conceived by the machine (age), the protagonist is reborn without identity, individuality, or background—the proper moment for his re-conception, when he no longer knows his name, where he was born, who he *was*. The pre-frontal lobotomy, minus knife and physical scars, is the contemporary, scientific method of brain-clean: his recapitulated history, once effaced, produces a nonman, an ironic *tabula rasa* identity. Once severed from his electric umbilical cord, he is emptied of tradition (in this sophisticated, psychological manner) almost as effectively as the enslaved African, torn ruthlessly from his land and raped of his past more than three hundred years earlier.

One flaw mars the machinery, however; it cannot turn out a completely computerized (non)man when even the most minuscule amount of humanity remains to touch him into life. This is much better illustrated in the original section deleted from *Invisible Man* and published separately as "Out of the Hospital and Under the Bar" in *Soon, One Morning* (1966). In an "Author's Note," Ellison explains:

> For those who would care to fit it back into *Invisible Man* let them start at the point where the explosion occurs in the paint factory, substitute the the following happenings, and leave them once the hero is living in Mary's hope.[9]

Mother Mary of Harlem, who finds the young man staggering out of the subway, springs rather unsatisfactorily from nowhere into the novel, but she helps him achieve rebirth in the original episode:

> When I awakened she stood looking down. Her newly straightened hair gleamed glossily in the intense light, her blue uniform freshly ironed and stiffly starched. Seeing me awake she shook her head and grinned. (Hill 1966, 244)

Without real knowledge of the machine's complexity, she partially releases him and restores his strength with a foul-tasting home remedy: "That stuff'll make a baby strong" (Hill 1966, 261). Through Mary and her urbanized black folk world, the protagonist moves toward an identity based on his gradual acceptance of the realities of the past: swallowing the past, no matter how galling, makes the present possible. The overtones of emasculation are still there, for it is quite clear that to Ellison this is the essence of the black experience in America.

"Out of the Hospital and Under the Bar" is one of the most effective, densely symbolic scenes Ellison has written and the exigencies of publication should not have forced its excision. It is similar but superior to the Golden Day episode and foreshadows the running riot scene that returns the narrator to his underground womb. In a Freudian serio-comic nightmare, the naked narrator runs and is chased through the labyrinthine passages of his mind, until he bursts newborn from the subterranean womb into Harlem:

> I rolled, looking into the faces of two women dressed in white. "Police! A naked man, a naked ....!" the woman screamed. "Police!" "Oh no! No!" called a woman who crouched against a building

front. "Not naked! Is he, Sis Spencer? Let's us be sure 'fore we call the cops. Wait'll I change my glasses."
"As ever he was born in the world!" (Hill 1966, 283)

Two nurse-like women attend this birth, but the protagonist himself has been the most active, experiencing the pangs of passage, expelling himself from the symbolically ambiguous orifice—a manhole—naked into a new world of consciousness. But he has run a long way, leaving behind bodies deadened by the machine (age); shocking whites with his nakedness; encountering another basement black whose life is a perpetual gamble; and slipping away from the straitjacket-bearing attendant who tries to fit him with an adjustable identity—"It'll fit, all right, it's endlessly adjustable" (Hill 1966, 273). The naked narrator, however, has slipped off *all* identities, theirs and his own, and is racing toward some intangible hope, the possibility of perception:

And I was conscious of being somehow different. It was not only that I had forgotten my name or that I had been processed in the machine, or even that I had taken Mary's medicine—but something internal. My thoughts seemed to be the thoughts of another. Impressions flashed through my mind, too fleeting and secretly meaningful to have been my own—whoever I was. And yet somehow they were. It was as though I had become capable of new powers of understanding. (Hill 1966, 274)

But the cellar of his mind is still cluttered with old memories, all of which he must traverse before he can be free:

"Why would he think of coming down here?"
"Probably some buried memory guided him. Perhaps this strange basement corresponds to the structure of his mind. . . ." (Hill 1966, 275)

"Out of the Hospital" is almost completely a running scene, but for the first time the protagonist has an awareness of the meaning of running. The runner is in a flight that has the dreamlike quality of double vision: standing back, he watches himself running through his own history, which is, in a sense, a history of the race in microcosm. The hospital scene in the novel has this quality, but with little of the dramatic impact of the deleted section. Ellison sustains this motion and suspense, reminiscent of the excitement of escape in the slave narrative, even to the inclusion of the pursuing hound. When the narrator finally arrives "Under the Bar," he blends into the blackness—"nigger in the coal locker"—until the dog and the men at his heels force him to thrust himself through the manhole. The section ends with the protagonist deciding to find "Old Mary," but in the meantime he has had an important encounter with a blind man in Harlem who bears a startling resemblance to his grandfather (from whom he cannot escape), and who also reminds him of Bledsoe, the briefcase, and part of his still undigested past: "Well, a young fellow has to keep moving . . ." (Hill 1966, 287).

"Out of the Hospital" is an artfully executed recapitulation section that will be used later, not so much as a structural device, but as contrast. The protagonist's running in the simulated riot is realistically, almost naturalistically, described and the outcome is reversed. The runner drops back through the manhole into the womb of the earth to be born again or finally buried. In this earlier episode, however, he is reborn into the bosom of the folk with a beginning recognition of and pride in his origins—essentially a new identity reshaped from the old. The old remedy, put together from herbs and recipes of the past, has given him strength to force himself out of the mechanical womb of an automated society that seeks to make automatons of men and to exploit their strength for its perpetuation. When he finally comes up for air, from the underground of past feelings and experiences, he finds himself in Harlem, the promised land that will not yield its promise. This he has yet to experience; now he is without fear, but also without illusions.

Most of his subsequent experiences in Harlem force him into the recognition that he cannot escape who he *was*: soul food ("I yam what I yam"); the dispossessed old southern folk; the "piece of early Americana" which Mary keeps in his room—"the cast iron figure of a very black, red-lipped and wide-mouthed Negro" (Ellison 1952, 242); the updated slave chain, a gift of Brother Tarp, another Running Man; Tod Clifton's Sambo doll; and finally that intangible part of himself that is permanently welded to his grandfather—"the cynical, disbelieving part" (Ellison 1952, 254). Yet, in Harlem he also takes on another shape, the identity handed him by the Brotherhood.

Ironically, the Brotherhood thinks of him as a new "Booker T. Washington," but he has already shed his illusions of ever assuming such an identity: "To hell with this Booker T. Washington business. I would do the work but I would be no one except myself—whoever I was" (Ellison 1952, 236). He finds, however, that his role of "Brother" carries with it ill-fitting masks that are repugnant to him: he is an Uncle Tom to Ras, a black stud to Emma, an opportunistic plotter to Brother Westrum (Rest Room), and eventually a traitor to the people in Harlem who trusted him. The latter mask he tries to rid himself of when Ras the Destroyer's men attempt to track him down. The Hollywood disguise he thinks he is assuming with shades "of a green glass so dark that it appeared black" metamorphoses him into Rinehart, a confidence man in the Melville tradition, a "confidencing sonofabitch":

Everybody knows Rinehart, and since he is so easily mistaken, it would seem that his is known to nobody. B. P. Rinehart—the B. for Bliss, the P. for Proteus—is a numbers runner; he would seem to be a nigger boy who has kept running but who has made a function of it, who somehow has come to own the track....[10]

Rinehart (the rind without the heart) is a progenitor of Kelley's Cooley Johnson (*dem*) where he becomes almost a folk hero, but Ellison sees Rinehart's nonidentity as a negative perspective for his protagonist. The epitome of the happy Proteus, his invisibility is essentially egoistic, conscienceless, asocial if not antisocial. He is a gambler, a briber, a lover (roles the protagonist will never master), a man who can cope with the shifting realities of the times because his own identity is fluid, unimpeded by the barriers of a functioning superego. Running is a way of life for him and invisibility his natural dress. Rinehart uses hiding, duplicity (and multiplicity)—all the old, inherited tactics of slave tradition—to make himself invisible in his various guises. Running is a logical necessity for his activities, amorous, ministerial, and criminal.

Running has become a way of life for the narrator, too, but its meaning remains ambiguous. Because he has neither a "smooth tongue" nor a "heartless heart," he is not at home in Rinehart's "hot world of fluidity," in the confidence game of life, even though its potential seems limitless. "You could actually make yourself anew," he thinks, just as Cross Damon had thought, but Ellison's protagonist finds the notion too frightening and confusing to contemplate: "And sitting there trembling I caught a brief glimpse of the possibilities posed by Rinehart's multiple personalities and turned away" (Ellison 1952, 377). Knowing of Rinehart's existence, however, is a salutary experience, and the narrator even thinks for a time that he can put it to use. But the Rinehart mask he dons, fortuitously does not fit when he tries to act the role. Rinehartism, which he finally equates with cynicism and charlatanism, is not his way and eventually he rejects it. What he does learn is that "somewhere between Rinehart and invisibility there were great potentialities" (Ellison 1952, 386).

Rejecting Rinehartism as an identity does not mean that the protagonist embraces invisibility. That final role is forced upon him by the blindness of others: Bledsoe, Norton, Emerson, Kimbro, Brockway, Jack, Hambro, even Mary. It was his role in the beginning ("the end was in the beginning"), only he did not recognize it. He *was* and yet *was not*, and somehow his recognition of nonbeing moves him toward a state of definition:

I was my experiences and my experiences were me, and no blind men, no matter how powerful they became, even if they conquered the world, could take that, or change one single itch, taunt, laugh, cry, scar, ache, rage or pain of it." (Ellison 1952, 383)

Blindness afflicted Bigger Thomas's world, preventing his humanity from becoming visible. Blindness afflicts Ellison's protagonist also. Barbee is completely blind, Jack half-blind, others symbolically blind. However, he is seen *through* whereas Bigger Thomas was not seen at all. Bigger's non-identity is fixed and immutable, like the black ghetto in which he lived, but the Invisible Man functions on a canvas of shifting planes, where his "unreality" is in the eye of the beholder: each person or group he encounters redefines him on the basis of what they want to see, what they think they see, or what they *insist* on seeing. He is reduced to the strange state of dubiety Ellison describes in *Shadow and Act*. "In our society it is not unusual for a Negro to experience a sensation that he does not exist in the real world at all."[11] Choosing to accept his past is a positive step toward self-definition for the protagonist of *Invisible Man*; it means exercising his will to reject the "unreality" of others and to affirm his own humanity—every "itch, taunt, laugh, cry, scar, ache, rage or pain of it."

Clutching the briefcase that contains his past (his Rineharts, his Brotherhood identification, the anonymous letter, Tod Clifton's doll, Tarp's leg chain), he runs back toward Harlem, toward some self that can only be found in the chaos of the riot, which, in a sense, symbolizes the chaos within himself. The briefcase is lost momentarily when he helps set fire to a tenement and he is panic stricken, but when he fumbles in it desperately to find any identity that will save him from hanging by Ras the Exhorter turned Ras the Destroyer, all are useless except the leg chain. First, he divests himself of the broken glasses (Rinehartism) and next, of his Brotherhood identity. "I am no longer their brother," he shouts, trying vainly to explain to Ras's feebly armed group that in their riotous, misdirected anger, they will destroy themselves. The crowd listens momentarily to the debate between reason and irrationality, but is in no mood to accept a definition of its own absurd role: "Use a nigger to catch a nigger." Ras in his blindness is eager to offer up a sacrificial lamb, and the crowd, as foolishly blindfolded as the boys in "battle royal," is eager to hang its scapegoat.

I was invisible, and hanging would not bring me to visibility, even to their eyes, since they wanted my death not for myself alone but for the chase

I'd been on all my life; because of the way I'd run, been run, chased, operated, purged—although to a great extent I could have done nothing else, given their blindness . . . and my invisibility. (Ellison 1952, 422)

The oppressed are, in the final analysis, as blind as the oppressors, who have staged another battle royal and egged them on to fight each other, this time in a death ring. But the Invisble Man refuses to take part in another fiasco, refuses to die for anyone else's absurdity, and when Ras shouts, "Hang him," he pins the Destroyer's jaws shut with his own ludicrous weapon, a spear. Tarp's leg chain and his own briefcase are the narrator's only weapons and he uses them against Ras's men (racists of his own race), as they try to impede his escape, in a final rejection of a protean shape he could never assume. The one-eyed brotherhood of false Jacks is wrong, but so is a pure black mask of inhumanity. What the protagonist has learned on his long and painful flight, the crowd cannot apprehend in a brief moment of revelation, even if his sacrificial death were to bring them one "bloody step closer to a definition of who they were" and of what he was and had been.

Ellison's protagonist has no martyr complex. He is not a godlike, heroic figure ready to sacrifice himself for the sins of humanity, black or white; he is unheroic modern man, fleeing from chaos toward a rational sense of order, which if it does not exist in the world, can exist at least in his own mind. When he returns to his underground womb (a circular journey if we include the "Out of the Hospital" sequence), it is to escape irrational forces in the shape of two white men armed with a baseball bat who want to wrest from him all that he has gained in experience—his briefcase. He alone can divest himself of those past identities, and he does, one by one, lighting his way to his underground future. But the underground life is not permanent: "Thus, having tried to give pattern to the chaos which lives within the pattern of your certainties, I must come out, I must emerge" (Ellison 1952, 438). His hibernation is over, the narrator tells us, the immobility that can be like death—total inaction, final invisibility. He does not know whether he will find death or life aboveground, and he is braced only by the certainty of his invisibility and the possibility of ours.

That possibility, and the narrator's sense of social responsibility, makes Ellison one of the few black writers whose Running Man most clearly reflects both positive *and* negative aspects of running, and whose protagonist epitomizes the experiences of both the black and white Running Man of the twentieth century. For Running Man *is* twentieth-century man, fleeing from invisibility (nonidentity) toward a visibility (identity) which he has at least some role in shaping. Invisibility in Ellison's novel is due not only to color, or its absence, but to the fact that such is the human condition, the fate of man impotent in the face of the powerful dehumanizing forces of contemporary society. Ellison's sense of the total community, implicit throughout the book, is explicit in the epilogue. In trying, as he does continually, to solve the conundrum of his grandfather's deathbed advice, the narrator comes close to a comprehension of the responsibility of the black man as a "center of knowing":

Was it that we of all, we, most of all, had to affirm the principle, the plan in whose name we had been brutalized and sacrificed—not because we would always be weak nor because we were afraid or opportunistic, but because we were older than they, in the sense of what it took to live in the world with others and because they exhausted in us, some—not much, but some—of the human greed and smallness, yes, and the fear and super-stition that had kept them running. (Ellison 1952, 433-434)

His understanding that "they're running too, running all over themselves" broadens his base of commitment to the real world of pattern and chaos, love and hate, black and white:

America is woven of many strands; I would recognize them and let it so remain. It's "winner take nothing" that is the great truth of our country or of any country. Life is to be lived, not controlled; and humanity is won by continuing to play in face of certain defeat. Our fate is to become one, and yet many. (Ellison 1952, 435)

The grandson learns from his experiences something that the grandfather was unable to learn from a life of denigration: "Weren't we *part of them* as well as apart from them and subject ot die when they died?"—the indis-soluble link of humanity.

Ellison's Running Man stems from both the tradition of the fugitive slave actually running for his life, and the larger literary tradition of the nineteenth century which saw the black man as a symbol of humanity. "This conception of the Negro as a symbol of Man," Ellison writes, "was organic to nineteenth-century literature. It occurs not only in Twain but in Emerson, Thoreau, Whitman and Melville...."[12] We have already noted the significance of the running men in *Huckleberry Finn*. Twain brings together the white and the black runner in a symbiotic relationship that exists outside the rigid pattern set for them by society; through that rela-tionship they both attain the kind of freedom neither had before: "In freeing Jim, Huck makes a bid to free himself of the conventionalized evil taken for civilization by the town."[13] Jim becomes that symbol of humanity for the nineteenth century that the Invisible Man is for the twentieth. Ellison sets him in the center of a dichotomy so that at every juncture of his life he is forced to answer questions never clearly posed, to identify himself in a world of nonreflecting mirrors, to define his existence in a society so sick with myopia that it is unable to assume his visibility, his humanity, as a matter of course.

If Ellison's Running Man is modern man, speaking in a generalized way for all of us, how can he also speak in a particularized way for the Afro-American, whose experiences we know are unique? For one thing, his flight is a creative recapitulation of black history in this country. His roots are in the plantation South; his aspirations move him toward the black southern college for "good niggers"; his move North parallels the Great Migration of the twenties and is fraught with disillusionment. Second, the reality of his life in America, especially his heritage of slavery, has made the experience of running not merely a gesture toward freedom but a flight for his life. This is literally true for Ellison's protagonist during the riot scene— a contemporary development—where he is hounded not only by whites but also by bellicose blacks. Third, his area of choice is severely limited. Unlike the runners in Fitzgerald, Salinger, Kerouac, and Updike, who, no matter how limited they are psychologically or monetarily, freely make the decision to run, the Invisible Man is usually precipitated into running by some "sin" he commits against the system. It is a satiric comment on the black man's experience in America, on the negative alternatives rather than clear choices with which he is usually confronted. Fourth, the geographic locations to which he can run are finely delineated. The back-to-nature frontier has disappeared for all twentieth-century running men, but the black runner has difficulty even fleeing the city for the suburbs. Wright's runners were circumscribed by the iron ring around the city to which they were linked by their race, for although their humanity was invisible, their color was not. The Invisible Man finds a northern home in Harlem, but when he drops out of society it is into an underground home, an ironic return of "the nigger to the coal pile." Ellison clearly understands how the black experience in America has shaped the black sensibility, how it has made the fictional as well as the actual life of the Afro-American different from that of his white counterpart:

Obviously the experiences of Negroes—slavery, the grueling and continuing fight for full citizenship since Emancipation, the stigma of color, the enforced alienation which constantly knifes into our natural identification with our country—have not been that of white Americans. And though as passionate believers in democracy Negroes identify themselves with the broader American ideals, their sense of reality springs, in part, from an

American experience which most white men not only have not had, but one with which they are reluctant to identify themselves even when presented in forms of the imagination.[14]

Is the ending of *Invisible Man* completely negative, as many critics have suggested? Only if we consider all flight negative. The protagonist's last venture into himself, like Thoreau's, is a successful leap into perception, a perception of his own identity and his own reality. What he has begun to learn above ground—that he could not return to Mary's, to the campus, to the Brotherhood, or home—he has assimilated emotionally during the hiatus underground. The knowledge needed to resume action has finally been exhumed to the level of consciousness, and he is ready to leave his hibernation—to return, as Ishmael does, to the shore—with his conflicts but also with his sense of humanity restored.

NOTES

1. Edwin Seaver, ed., *Cross Section* (New York, 1944), pp. 58-102.
2. "The Politics of Ellison's Booker: *Invisible Man* as Symbolic History," *Chicago Review* XIX (1966-67): 25.
3. Ralph Ellison, *Invisible Man* (New York, 1952), p. 11. Further citations will be in the text.
4. Carl Milton Hughes, *The Negro Novelist* (New York, 1953), p. 272.
5. James Baldwin, *Nobody Knows My Name* (New York, 1961), p. 5.
6. David Galloway, *The Absurd Hero in American Fiction* (Austin, Texas, 1966), p. 141.
7. Jonathan Baumbach, "Nightmare of a Native Son: Ralph Ellison's *Invisible Man*," *Critique* VI, no. 1 (Spring 1963): 57.
8. Ralph Ellison, *Shadow and Act* (New York, 1964), p. 105.
9. Herbert Hill, ed., *Soon, One Morning: New Writing by American Negroes*, 1940-1962 (New York, 1966), p. 243. Further citations will be in the text.
10. Marcus Klein, *After Alienation: American Novels in Mid-Century* (Cleveland, 1962), p. 133. Klein also notes that "Ellison himself has compared Rinehart to the Confidence Man. *Paris Review* interview, p. 70" (p. 302).
11. Ellison, *Shadow and Act*, p. 304.
12. Ibid., p. 32.
13. Ibid., p. 32.
14. Ibid., p. 225.

6. THE PASSIVE RESISTANTS

"You cant escape, there's no where to go"[1]

Ellison's seminal book set the pattern of ambiguity for the Running Man metaphor, his *Invisible Man* establishing a literary precedent for writers of the sixties. The protagonist as Running Man was not only a reflection of the times but a creative projection of the future. If the "Negro is America's metaphor," as Richard Wright has said, then it is valid for us to assume that the Running Man is one of the black writer's most effective metaphors, the symbol through which he has been able to express his view of America's agony. In both fiction and drama, Afro-American writers since Ellison—men like William Kelley, Douglas Turner Ward and Ronald L. Fair—have used running as one method of articulating their conception of the black experience in America.

In Kelley's first novel, *A Different Drummer*, running is above all a positive act of renunciation. The book takes its title from the concluding chapter of *Walden* and is in fact a reversion to that early period of civil disobedience based on the "higher law" of conscience:

If a man does not keep pace with his companions, perhaps it is because he hears a different drummer. Let him step to the music which he hears, however measured or far away.[2]

Implicit in Thoreau's withdrawal from the world was his "rejection of a materialistic society."[3] Tucker Caliban, Kelley's protagonist in *A Different Drummer*, rejects the society into which he was born the grandson of a slave, and the state in which he has lived all his life. Moving purposefully, at his own pace, he is in some ways reminiscent of the Emersonian self-reliant man whom Thoreau epitomizes:

And truly it demands something godlike in him who has cast off the common motives of humanity, and has ventured to trust himself for a taskmaster. High be his heart, faithful his will, clear his sight, that he may in good earnest be doctrine, society, law, to himself, that simple purpose may be to him as strong as iron necessity is to others.[4]

Tucker is the great-grandson of an almost legendary African who escaped from Auction Square in New Marsails after the first Willson, of a long line of prestigious Willsons, purchased him directly off a slaver and tried unsuccessfully to subdue him. Kelley's novel deals with the Willson and Caliban descendants unto the third and fourth generation and shows their ironically interdependent existence in an "East South Central State in the Deep South . . . bounded on the north by Tennessee; east by Alabama; south by the Gulf of Mexico; west by Mississippi."[5]

This fantasy in real dress begins with an excerpt from "The Thumb-Mail Almanac, 1961," describing the state's past history, and more important, its recent history:

In June 1957, for reasons yet to be determined, all the state's Negro inhabitants departed. Today, it is unique in being the only state in the Union that cannot count even one member of the Negro race among its citizens. (Kelley 1959, 2)

What follows is an unfolding of the mystery that surrounds Tucker Caliban's act of renunciation, the catalyst that precipitates the black exodus.

The three major characters are Tucker, David Willson, a young idealistic southerner, and Bennett Bradshaw, a northern black intellectual whom David meets at a New England college—obviously Harvard, a school Kelley knows from experience. Together they plan to reshape the world; instead, the world reshapes them. After a number of chastening experiences as a progressive journalist, David returns to Willson "Swells" to become a rent collector for his father, an heir to the life that was anathema to him. In the process he becomes a bitter, unloving husband and a distant father. David's loss of idealism is matched by Bennett's, who becomes the Reverend B. T. Bradshaw, founder of the Resurrected Church of the Black Jesus Christ of America, Inc., a self-ordained minister of the black gospel: "organized like the Marines, the Black Jesuits have a doctrine which is a mixture of *Mein Kampf, Das Kapital,* and the Bible" (Kelley 1959, 194).

Using Tucker as the moral focus of the novel, Kelley is able to comment on the extremes symbolized by Bradshaw and David Willson: the black intellectual who is unscrupulous in his bid for power and whose leadership is made obsolete by the innate power that exists in Tucker, and in every man, who finds it in himself to seize the day; and the decent white southerner who is motivated by an honest desire to redress grievances and a conviction that the mind of the South can be changed, but who is impotent because he lacks the courage to initiate change. Willson's life proves Emerson's contention that "inaction is cowardice"; Willson's orientation, like Bradshaw's, is intellectual; Tucker's is not. Bradshaw knows this without ever having seen Caliban:

"We're not talking about a sophisticate drawing inspiration from Plato; we're talking about an ignorant southern Negro. We're not talking about the new, complex ideas: the unique thunderbolts of thought that come to men of genius. We're talking about the old ideas, the simple ones, the fundamental ideas that perhaps we've overlooked, or never even tried. But Tucker Caliban cannot overlook them; he has just discovered them." (Kelley 1959, 138)

Tucker's ability to act and his courage to act alone set him apart from both Bradshaw and Willson. What's more, he is closer to the truth of the old, fundamental ideas that Bradshaw extols because his life has remained simple. His life is not veneered with the new and complex, the failure of which is represented partially by Bradshaw and partially by Tucker's wife Bethrah, a refined and educated southern black woman who can talk civil rights but cannot act to attain them. Tucker does not look to the college-educated black of southern or northern extraction for leadership. Nor does he have to be admonished "to pursue *his own* way, and not his father's or his mother's, or his neighbor's instead."[6]

The "drummer" passage quoted by Kelley from the conclusion of *Walden* is preceded by an equally significant one from the opening chapter of that book:

The greater part of what my neighbors call good I believe in my soul to be bad, and if I repent of anything, it is very likely to be my good behavior. What demon possessed me that I behaved so well? (Kelley 1959, 11)

For Tucker, the first sign that he has behaved too well too long is the death of his grandfather, old John Caliban, whose whole life was spent as a menial at Willson "Swells." John draws his last breath at the back of a bus in direct view of a *Colored* sign—ironically, a man who had kept his place to the end of the line. Tucker stalks out of the funeral service when the preacher eulogizes the old man for all the sacrifices he made: "Sacrifice be damned!" Two months later he buys seven acres of farmland from David Willson, a piece of land on which Tucker's people had worked as slaves and then employees from the time of the first Caliban. This is Tucker's primary act of will, the first unhesitating step of the Running Man who turns his back on "good" behavior.

The fact that David sells the land to Tucker surprises his family and angers the white tenants, for the Willson plantation is a remnant of the state's proud antebellum past; no part of it has ever left white Willson hands. The farm has a different symbolic value for Tucker; it means that the last Caliban has been indentured to the last Willson. Tucker's and Bethrah's son will be his own master. However, Tucker is a Running Man, and owning land that he considers rightfully his becomes a means, not an end. The following spring he destroys the farm. Step by step, he salts the land, shoots all his animals, hacks down General Willson's favorite tree and chops to pieces DeWitt Willson's imported clock, brought over on the slaver that sailed into New Marsails with Tucker's African ancestor. Then, after gathering his family together, he sets the house ablaze and walks away. This act of renunciation of all that the plantation stands for sets him free; it also sets the other blacks on the road until the state is depleted by one-third of its population.

A Different Drummer is the dream fantasy of the childlike innocent who looks on as the once powerful grieve or rage at his untimely departure. Kelley's powerless whites react to the enigma of the departure in various ways, some predictable, others unaccountable: the ignorant continue in their stupid belligerence, climaxing in the lynching of Bradshaw; those, like Harry Leland, who have some inherent decency try to find the answer in the present; others, like old man Harper, search for it in the past, as if the blood of that first African runaway who tried to free every slave in bondage has finally "started to itch" in the veins of his descendant. [7] Only the Willson family understands that Tucker has broken the pattern of the past by rejecting all the tangible symbols of black servitude. He takes to the road in a movement toward freedom, but there is of course no real place for the Running Man to go, no "promised land" in the North, no new frontier in twentieth-century America. However, the act of running is the symbolic act of striving implicit in the "drummer" quotation. What action a man takes, Thoreau said earlier, must come out of his commitment to himself. It need not be successful in its outcome, but it must be undertaken from principle born of conscience. His desire to commit himself must be so strong that his conscience would suffer a mortal blow were he to remain uncommitted. The kind of individual, even anarchic, action Thoreau took in refusing allegiance to the state was not precipitate. Nor is

Tucker's decision to dissociate himself from Kelley's mythical state a precipitate one. It rises out of an unshakable commitment to himself. The music which the self-reliant man hears is on a very high frequency indeed.

Kelley's problem in *A Different Drummer* is not so much to make credible the actions of Tucker's followers (this is, after all, a fantasy) as to convince the reader that his fictional Thoreau *is* that rare man of such acute and selective hearing that he can successfully drown out the noise of his fettered past in order to hear his own soul. Clearly, at this juncture, the black and white experience separate. To initiate voluntarily the ascetic life of denial and austerity in order to put oneself in touch with nature and the divine spirit, and ultimately with oneself, is the voluntary act of a free man. Denial and austerity, however, have been *imposed* on Tucker and on all the Calibans from without, by a superannuated social system that is indefensible on any level. Unfortunately, perhaps, we have come to associate deprivation with the kind of sociology so finely delineated by Richard Wright in *Black Boy* and *Native Son*: deprivation begets fear/anger/violence in an unending circuit of pain. Tucker is, then, in one sense a twentieth-century anachronism—a romantic hero, unlettered, unschooled in the art of leadership and motivated almost entirely from within. He has none of the self-destructive impulses we have learned to equate with the psychology of the deprived; he is neither sadistic nor masochistic. When he acts, he is impelled by the dictates of his own conscience, and when he destroys, he destroys *things*, real chattel (animals, trees, land); property, not people, not himself.

To compound the problem of credibility, Kelley only allows the reader to see Tucker from the outside through the eyes of whites. A chapter is devoted to each Willson and the rest to the townspeople. The book begins with the destruction of the farm, a destruction witnessed by thirty-odd men of the town, indolent whites who spend most of their time lounging about the porch of the town store in Sutton. As the story progresses, their anxiety increases, for they finally come to realize that they have lost their last black scapegoat. Bradshaw's lynching is made to seem the final act of violence in a drama several hundred years old. However, Kelley's attitude toward the southerners is in one way a romantic reversion.[8] With the exception of Harry Leland and Mr. Harper, the "good" whites are represented by the Willsons. A streak of chivalry found in the old, aristocratic family does not abide anywhere else. The poor whites, like Leland, are essentially weak and ineffectual, so there is little hope that they can ameliorate the situation at their level. The implication is that change comes to those who have had some contact with Tucker's quiet strength. Harry Leland's young son, who has known Tucker all his life, refuses to believe ill of him and represents, no doubt, the slender thread of hope for his generation; while the Willsons, who have been touched by the Calibans in every generation, seem in the final analysis to be the only southern whites capable of real change—a romantic idea that Kelley does not entertain in his much more realistic and bitter novel, *dem.*

Tucker has the solitary nature of all running men—Ellison's Invisible Man, Wright's outsider, the westerner, Thoreau, Ishmael, Huck Finn—but he bears an interesting resemblance to the latter. Eliot, in his introduction to *The Adventures of Huckleberry Finn,* distinguishes between the independence of Huck and the independence of the "typical or symbolic American Pioneer"[9] (i.e., Leatherstocking), for Huck's existence questions most of the values of American society: "He is as much an affront to the 'pioneer spirit' as he is to 'business enterprise.'" The analogy here is clear. Tucker's existence questions the values of both white and black America; his actions are an affront to the status quo of the sick South and the not much healthier North. Eliot also insists that Huck "must come from nowhere and be bound for nowhere." Tucker doesn't know where he comes from because his slave ancestors were uprooted from a land he has never seen and never expects to see, and he is of course bound for nowhere. Like Huck, "who has no beginning and no end," he can only disappear. His disappearance and that of the other blacks, however, is into a kind of invisibility that is itself an identity; that is, they become visibly significant only by virtue of their absence.

Huck's disappearance, Eliot says, is accomplished "by bringing forward another performer, Tom Sawyer, to obscure the disappearance in a cloud of whimsicalities." In *A Different Drummer* the other performer is Bennett Bradshaw, but his is the role of victim and the cloud that screens Tucker and the black "secessionists" is a cloud of violence. Bradshaw's death obscures the departure of the passive resistants (they are like those long lines of civil rights marchers of the fifties who have all but disappeared), but it is not intended to obscure the reality of the southern "way of life." Violence, which Bradshaw preached as leader of the Black Jesuits, is the South's answer to passive resistance. It cannot tolerate overt criticism of its social system, dramatized here by the defection of the blacks. Beneath the comedy in *Huckleberry Finn* and the fantasy in *A Different Drummer* is the suggestion of ultimate tragedy.

Although society will always resist change, some individuals will inevitably resist the status quo by refusing to participate in society. The entire black population of Douglas Turner Ward's mythical southern town refuses to participate in that town's activities for twenty-four hours. In *Day of Absence* (1965), Ward's one-act satirical fantasy in whiteface, the white population is left in a state of impotent frenzy when the blacks vanish. Apparently without benefit of a leader even by indirection, like

Tucker Caliban, they depart as one Running Man, en masse, and their disappearance is inexplicable. The day of 100 percent absenteeism brings about the town's near collapse, for it cannot survive without its "mammies" in the kitchen and in the nursery, and its "Nigras" who perform as "Mop and Brush Men," all menials in residence. The South, as Mayor Henry R. E. Lee knows, "has always been glued together by the uninterrupted presence of its darkies."[10]

As the cock crows on a new day, Rastus shuffles on in the last scene. The only black to appear on stage in his native hue, he is a combination of "Stepin Fetchit, Willie Best, Nicodemus, B. McQueen and all the rest rolled into one" (Ward 1966, 57). The corner crackers, Clem and Luke, try to question him about the day of absence, but his answers are equivocal. "Tuesday . . . huh? That's sump'um . . . I . . . don't . . . remember . . . missing . . . a day . . . Mr. Luke . . . but I guess you right" (Ward 1966, 57). With a blank face and perfect aplomb, he follows the deathbed advice of the old grandfather in *Invisible Man:* "I want you to overcome 'em with yeses, undermine 'em with grins, agree 'em to death and destruction, let 'em swoller you till they vomit or bust wide open."[11] Luke accuses Rastus of lying but Rastus behaves in the time-honored tradition of the obsequious, yea-saying black, nurtured in the residue of slave culture—the masked black con man. Josiah Henson, Frederick Douglass, and other slave narrators learned to be adept at guile and deceit. Henson managed on numerous occasions to get his hands on "stray chickens" and found "first-rate tricks to dodge work."[12] In his autobiography Douglass commented on his own stealing:

In the case of my master, it was only a question of removal—the taking his meat out of one tub and putting it into another; the ownership of the meat was not affected by the transaction. At first he owned it in the *tub* and last he owned it in me.[13]

Ward's view of what would actually happen to southern society should the black population leave is not too far from Kelley's. A certain kind of chaos descends on the mythical locale of each. Ward's handling is for the most part broadly farcical, a minstrel show in reverse, while Kelley projects a quite different atmosphere. Both men criticize southern life through the metaphor of the Running Man acting, as he rarely does, en masse. If this is the white man's dream—to be rid of the black—fine. They remove him and reveal white society for what it is—dependent upon the black man for its maintenance, its sustenance, and its lies.

Ronald L. Fair's *Many Thousand Gone* (1965), which he calls "An American Fable," is cast in the satirical fantasy pattern set by Kelley and

Ward. In this case, however, the black community, finally on the rise, goes beyond passive resistance to emancipate their putative emancipators and then burn down the county. The passive resistants, once mobilized, take their revenge and run—three thousand strong.

Fair's locale is a tiny mythical county in Mississippi, so isolated that the blacks, unaware of changes in the outside (real) world, are still enslaved. Ironically, the novel is a kind of updated slave narrative, for the blacks still exist in almost nineteenth-century conditions. Even the title is taken from a pre-emancipation spiritual:

> No more auction block for me,
> No more, no more;
> No more auction block for me,
> Many thousand gone.

Many thousand have gone from the South, but Jacobs County is guarded and run by the sheriff and its one plantation owner, the benign Mr. Jacobs—that unbeatable combination of benevolent owner and vicious overseer. Together they keep the blacks at work in the fields, unpaid, uneducated, and immobilized by fear. They symbolize the millions of docile southern blacks who, before the 1950's, accepted conditions not too different from those that prevailed before the Civil War. Their submissiveness, according to Fair's satirical vision, is the consequence of a plan of masterful deceit, the wholesale duping (through legal, political, and economic chicanery) of the majority by the careful collusion of the minority. By 1920, in Fair's fantasied town:

Fewer than a dozen Negroes who had personal knowledge of the Civil War remained, and in time even they forgot that they had been emancipated. Slavery to them was better than death. They ceased to resist. The guards dwindled away to one sheriff and three deputies, and the white people of Jacobs County were often heard to say, "Our niggers are the freest niggers in the world."[14]

The Negroes of Jacobs County are "free" to become a part of the white community in various unspecified ways. Black girls, for example, are free to mother the child of any white boy who feels inclined to grant her the privilege. In fact, that privilege is so magnanimously bestowed that there are practically no pure black firstborn babies in Jacobs County. However, the blacks of Jacobs County are proud people, proud not to be white. In fact:

It was their practice to honor the first-born child of a first-born child regardless of sex, because these were the only children believed to be pure of race. No one remembered how the custom started, but down the years it had become firmly established, and they continued to celebrate joyously for the increasingly rare first-borns who were genuinely Negro." (Fair 1965, 11-12).

Many precautions had to be taken to protect their firstborn girls against accidental or purposefully planned fun on the part of the fun-loving white boys of Jacobs County. In fact, the first Running Man of the story kills three white boys while attempting to protect his girlfriend from rape. "All Clay knew was that he had to get north so he could stop running" (Fair 1965, 16). Of the three running men (perhaps in the language of the book they should be called fugitive slaves) in *Many Thousand Gone*, only one is actually heard from again. The blacks who survive the lynching terror after the death of the white boys never know whether Clay escaped, but they think he did: " 'After all,' one of the old men said, 'if they had done caught that boy they sho' nuf woulda done brought him back here so's we could see what they had done to him' " (Fair 1965, 17).

Jesse is the second Running Man. After he fathers the last pure black baby and attends his wife's funeral, he declines to be mauled by the deputy sheriff for refusing to move out of the deputy's way:

Jesse caught his arm and snapped his wrist with a loud crack. The deputy's eyes bulged with shock and disbelief, and he screamed in pain. Jesse raised the club and came down on his skull with powerful, rapid strokes. The deputy fell to the ground dead. Jesse would have to leave Jacobsville. He would have to run away, and although he was willing to take the baby, Granny Jacobs wouldn't hear of it. (Fair 1965, 22)

Granny Jacobs is unofficial matriarch in Jacobsville. As with the slaves of old, her last name is acquired from the plantation owner, one of those traditions of slavocracy preserved by this flowering Mississippi utopia. She and the preacher keep the black community together, working, singing, and worshiping. Granny smuggles the "Black Prince" out of Jacobsville so that he can live to grow up, even staging a fake funeral for the child. Little Jesse is the last Running Man to escape from Jacobsville, but it is clear that through Jesse (biblical father of a king) there is hope for the race.

Through the years Granny gets messages about Jesse through Preacher Harris, the only black person in town who is allowed to receive mail. ("Ain't one out a thousand niggers can read.") One day he comes to her with the news that Jesse has written a book about Jacobsville, and the real trouble begins when Granny surreptitiously sends for a copy of *Ebony*. The magazine, with its stories and pictures of Jesse and the good life in the

North, is the catalyst for change in Jacobsville. The whites are incredulous, but the illiterate blacks believe what they can see if not read:

The Negro magazine stirred up more excitement than the white people in Jacobs County had seen in years. The day after it arrived an angry [white] crowd gathered on the steps of the courthouse and demanded to see it. Some of the men refused to believe that such a magazine existed. Others felt that even if it did exist, Negroes surely didn't live as well as the magazine said. "It's a plot by them northern nigger-lovers. They're just trying to turn our niggers against us," one man said. (Fair 1965, 63-64)

Granny Jacobs and Preacher Harris summon up courage to write to the President of their feudal conditions, and Jacobs County gets its first federal investigators. The postal inspector manages to get rid of the postmaster, who has been paying his black employees (non-civil service) $1.00 a week, before the backlash begins. Then the nightriders go to work. First they mutilate three black girls, and then they go after Granny Jacobs and Preacher Harris.

The "Mammy" and the "Preacher" are conservative southern black institutions, but passive resistance and civil disobedience in the South were born in the church, and the black woman marched bravely in the front ranks of the civil rights marches.[15] Ronald Fair recognizes these two, to some extent; after all, Granny is responsible for smuggling Jesse out of Jacobsville, and Jesse communicates news of the outside world to the preacher. Little changes, however, until Josh, the sheriff's disenchanted "black boy," gets his people together and burns down the county. The law, represented by the federal marshal and the postal inspector, is completely hamstrung by the racist sheriff:

The vulgar, illiterate sheriff had outwitted the entire United States government because all the time he had known something they didn't know. He knew he was at war with the Yankee forces; he knew he was fighting the same war his great-grandfather had fought. (Fair 1965, 106)

The sheriff confines the two government men to jail for "safekeeping"; the irony of legal justice in the South is that the law is locked up if it interferes with the rights of the white minority.

Unlike the shades of evil among the whites in *A Different Drummer*, the whites in Ronald Fair's fabled world are unrelievedly vulgar and despicable. They are not incensed at the possibility of losing the black population; in fact, they are quite willing to annihilate the race in one murderous orgy when they find that the government has the temerity to interfere with their folkways. Violence on a massive scale does not repel them. They decide to "roast Granny and Preacher Harris alive, slowly, as they would barbecue a hog, and then they were going to destroy every single possession owned by any Negro in Jacobs County" (Fair 1965, 107). Josh, the fighter, however, manages to subvert their plan. He pulls his people together into a fighting force, sets the town on fire and then hurries to the jail where, in a final ironic gesture, he sets "his emancipators free." Clearly the law, however well-intentioned, is not going to help blacks out of their twentieth-century enslavement. Nor is passive resistance anything but a holding action: "These people, who had never known the meaning of the word resistance, were marching to Granny's house to protect her from the white men" (Fair 1965, 88). Granny's only real protection comes, however, when the blacks meet violence with violence.

The Running Man in *Many Thousand Gone* is both anachronistic fugitive slave and the black man who proves the race up North by his brilliant example. Blacks here are escapees from a primitive present in search of a civilized existence, the opposite of those nineteenth-century runners who fled from a civilization that restricted individual freedom. These black running men are determined to seek freedom for the entire race; theirs is a social, collective vision. In Fair's not-so-fictional world, however, the black *fighter* unlocks the door of injustice. Running, for this protagonist, is more aggression than escape, aggression born of a new perception of black reality. Josh symbolizes the passive resistant on the road to militancy. He no longer rejects violence, but uses it as a tool in the struggle for life.

The act of running for Ward, Kelley, and Fair is, then, essentially social rather than solitary. The runners act en masse, even where their action is short-lived, as in *Day of Absence*. Kelley's vision of the Running Man in *A Different Drummer* is a rather straightforward Emersonian view. His characters' running is more controlled and less a mark of alienation than that of Ronald Fair's characters. Running for Tucker Caliban is in fact the demonstration of a principled position. For the desperate blacks under Josh's leadership it is exchanging those ethical imperatives that ostensibly actuate the dominant society for a whole new set of values not formulated in terms of the "general" social good. Nevertheless, it is social in a very real sense. Fair's satirical fantasy, *Many Thousand Gone*, reflects more vividly the changing tenor of the times, although Arthur Davis places both novels in the "neo-protest tradition."[16] For all practical purposes, the passive phase of the civil rights movement came to an end in the mid-sixties. The new militancy bred a new mood in many writers, including William Kelley, whose later novel, *dem*, reflects this divergent trend. For some, like Baraka, the anti-integrationist mood needed no impetus. The Running Man continues his metaphorical existence in the later work of these and other writers, and his actions take on new, positive connotations. Running as escape is gradually displaced by running as a subtle act of aggression.

NOTES

1. LeRoi Jones, "Jitterbugs," in *Dark Symphony: Negro Literature in America*, ed. James A. Emanuel and Theodore L. Gross (New York, 1968), p. 516.
2. Henry David Thoreau, *Writings*, Manuscript Edition (Boston, 1906) vol. II, 358-359.
3. Charles Anderson, *The Magic Circle of Walden* (New York, 1968), p. 57.
4. Ralph Waldo Emerson, *Essays* (New York, 1903), p. 26.
5. William Melvin Kelley, *A Different Drummer* (New York, 1959), p. 1. Further citations will be in the text.
6. Thoreau, *Writings*, vol. II p. 79.
7. I was told by the poet Robert Hayden that the myth of the Flying African inspired his poem, "O Daedalus, Fly Away Home." There is a quality in Kelley's prodigious African which is reminiscent of that mythical hero of black folklore who had only to spread his arms to fly away home (see "All God's Chillen Had Wings," *The Book of Negro Folklore*, pp. 62-65). Although the ancestor of the Calibans does not have (or has lost) the ability to fly, he has that instinctive resistance to bondage which the Flying African demonstrated by his refusal to stand still and be maltreated. The fable-fantasy of running men and the disappearing race in *A Different Drummer, Day of Absence*, and *Many Thousand Gone* recalls slavery's folklore tradition of the "flying man."
8. The great W. E. B. DuBois would probably not see this as romantic reversion. In *The Souls of Black Folk* (1903) he does in fact set up a paradigm which may have suggested itself to Kelley: "Even the attitude of the Southern whites toward the blacks is not, as so many assume, in all cases the same; the ignorant Southerner hates the Negro, the workmen fear his competition, the money-makers wish to use him as a laborer, some of the educated see a menace in his upward development, while others—usually the sons of the masters—wish to help him to rise" (p. 52).
9. T. S. Eliot, Introduction, in Mark Twain, *The Adventures of Huckleberry Finn*, The Cresset Press edition (London, 1950), p. xiv. Subsequent quotations in the text are all from p. xvi of this essay.
10. Douglas Turner Ward, *Happy Ending and Day of Absence* (New York, 1966), p. 51. Further citations will be in the text.
11. Ralph Ellison, *Invisible Man* (New York, 1952), pp. 13-14.
12. Quoted by Charles H. Nichols, *Many Thousand Gone: The Ex-Slaves' Account of Their Bondage and Freedom* (Leiden, Netherlands, 1963), p. 78.
13. Frederick Douglass, *My Bondage and My Freedom* (New York, 1855), p. 189.
14. Ronald L. Fair, *Many Thousand Gone* (New York, 1965), p. 6. Further citations will be in the text.
15. Ted Shine's "Grandmother," Mrs. Grace Love (in his play *Contribution*, first produced by the Negro Ensemble Company in 1969) takes civil disobedience out of the hands of the amateurs. She doesn't march with her militant grandson, but she eliminates the opposition through her special brand of black power: she bakes death into her cornbread so that Sheriff Morrison (and others) literally die of "love." The young have mastered the tactics of confrontation, but they are mere babes in the art of deception. This "granny" takes her place in the front lines of the struggle for freedom.
16. Arthur P. Davis, "Trends in Negro American Literature," in *Dark Symphony: Negro Literature in America* (New York, 1968), p. 524.

7. THE YOUTHFUL RUNNER

"Legs mean more than hands, so I gives them more attention. If you can run, you're O.K."[1]

The literary precursor of the boy runner is Huckleberry Finn, whose immediate twentieth-century white heir is Holden Caulfield, the prep-school fugitive and escapee from social sham. These two have many things in common, as critics have pointed out. They are both nonconformists who, like most running men, pursue their individual paths as outsiders; they both object to the restraints of society and are intent on personal freedom; they refuse to accept the social identity forced upon them and seek an identity of their own; and because they are essentially realists, they are able to penetrate society's sham and pretense. In fact, their experience as travelers on the road becomes a criticism of American life.[2]

The disappearance of the frontier has forced the boy runner back into a society that is inimical to him, or into an institution to contemplate his "maladjustment," as Holden does. While Huck could escape "sivilizing," Holden

is revealed as telling us his narrative from an institution of some kind—psychiatric, we are led to suspect—having been trapped by the people who want to "sivilize" him.[3]

Running, however, as we have seen, is not easily arrested, and for the black boy runner in particular it assumes varying shades of ambiguity. Imamu Baraka, William Kelley, and Claude Brown deal with youthful runners whose stories are as redolent with social criticism as those of Huck and

97

Holden. However, the kind of running each does is as much in contrast to the manner of Huck and Holden as it is similar. For some it is positive, a search for identity or a sense of community and an attempt to escape the stigma of society's ubiquitous epithet, "black boy." For others, it is a negative reflex, a way of "dropping out" of life. At times, running is closer to the con man criminality of more mature runners, with the difference that the youthful runner enjoys the pre-adult status of the not-yet-hardened confidence man.

Claude Brown is one of a long line of real and fictional ghetto youths[4]—including Julian Mayfield's "Steely" (*The Long Night*, 1958), Ronald Fair's Wilford Robinson (*Hog Butcher*, 1966), Kelley's Mance Bedlow in "The Life You Save," and Baraka's nameless runner in "A Chase"— and his autobiography, *Manchild in the Promised Land*, is written in ghetto vernacular. The pungent language of Harlem reflects the personality of "Sonny," Brown's persona, as the language of Huck and Holden reflects their personalities and milieu. What Charles Kaplan says about the speech employed by Twain and Salinger is applicable to Brown:

The slangy, idiomatic, frequently vulgar language which Twain and Salinger put in the mouths of their heroes is remarkable for the clarity of the self-portraits that emerge, as well as for the effortless accuracy of the talk itself.[5]

We can see in *Manchild* the difference between what may be called a totally creative projection of character and language and admittedly "straight" autobiography. Brown's ear is superb, and he has been able to transmit the street to the page with almost perfect pitch. *Manchild*, as Hobart Jarrett points out, "is a study in Harlem dialect."[6]

Sonny is the offspring of those disenchanted runners, seasoned in Richard Wright's South, who came North looking for the "promised land." They are southern sharecroppers:

the poorest people of the South who poured into New York City during the decade following the Great Depression. These migrants were told that unlimited opportunity for prosperity existed in New York and that there was no "color problem" there. They were told that Negroes lived in houses with bathrooms, electricity, running water, and indoor toilets.[7]

But the North was no New Canaan; it was a "slum ghetto," a cage set down in the city from which few escaped. And what happened to the children of these disillusioned southern black pilgrims? They "inherited the total lot of their parents—the disappointments, the anger. To add to their misery, they had little hope of deliverance. For where does one run to when he's already in the promised land?" (Brown 1965, 8).

The children of these southern immigrants are much like the children of early twentieth-century immigrants from western and eastern Europe, like Dreiser's Germans and Gold's Jews. They have no rapport with their parents who, ignorant of city life, are still steeped in rural southern ways and superstitions. The religion and folkways of "down home" were meaningless to Claude Brown:

While Daddy was still trying to beat me into a permanent conversion, Mama was certain that somebody had worked roots on me. She was writing to all her relatives in the South for solutions, but they were only able to say, "that boy must have been born with the devil in him." (Brown 1965, 21).

What horrified his parents most was that "Sonny" began to learn the "fine arts" of the street before he had been in school long enough to learn to read. He was such an apt pupil that

the neighborhood prophets began making prophecies about my life-span. . . .They all had me dead, buried, and forgotten before my twenty-first birthday. These predictions were based on false tales of policemen shooting at me, on truthful tales of my falling off a trolley car into the midst of oncoming automobile traffic while hitching a ride, and also on my uncontrollable urge to steal. There was much justification for these prophecies. By the time I was nine years old, I had been hit by a bus, thrown into the Harlem River (intentionally), hit by a car, severely beaten with a chain. And I had set the house afire. (Brown 1965, 21)

Claude's early education, although informal, was highly specialized. Danny was his best tutor at hookey, Butch at ringing cash registers, Buddy at "catting" (staying up all night), Knoxie at dancing and making zip guns. Bubba and Mr. Jimmy tutored him in sartorial excellence and the confidence game,[8] and his father was an expert at drinking, violence, and religion from the bottle. Like Huck, "Sonny Boy" did not have to leave home to learn the meaning of violence. His father and grandfather were both known for their irascibility. Sonny reacts to his father's brutality—beatings with a belt, ironing cord, or stick—in much the same way as Huck: he avoids it whenever possible. (Later he even comes to understand his father's terrible frustrations.) "Catting" was one method of avoidance: "Before long, I was catting regularly, staying away from home for weeks at a time. Sometimes the cops would pick me up and take me to a Children's Center" (Brown 1965, 21). The procedure was for the Children's Center to inform his parents, but often by the time his mother came to pick him up, he was on the run again.

Unlike Richard Wright, Sonny as a child is surrounded by affection, if not understanding: his sisters try to protect him from their father's beatings; his younger brother Pimp admires and respects him; and his mother loves him although his behavior confounds her. And he has a real fondness and attachment for his mother. Unlike other runners, young and old, Claude feels no compulsion to escape that "monster," woman. His running is at first a rebellion against the generation *and* the plantation gap; his flight from the down-home past that still grips his family: their ignorance, superstition, fear. And the appalling narrowness of their lives:

Liquor, religion, sex, and violence—this was all that life had been about to them. And a prayer that the right number would come out, that somebody would hit the sweepstakes or get lucky. It seemed as though if I had stayed in Harlem all my life, I might have never known that there was something else. (Brown 1965, 281)

At thirteen, Claude is shot in the stomach while stealing sheets from a clothesline, and his trips to Warwick, a bucolic reform school, begin. His education at Warwick is even more sophisticated than the one he acquired in the streets. He learns how to pick locks and cross wires for easy car theft, pick pockets, roll reefers, cut drugs, and boost weak pot with embalming fluid: "We all came out of Warwick better criminals." And when he does come out, Johnny D, Mr. Jimmy, and Reno bring him up to date on the confidence game.[9] Reno "was a good con man, one of the best I'd ever met. He started teaching me how to con cats out of goods, how to shake down prostitutes by pretending you were the law," and how to "work the Murphy" (fake pandering).

Claude's restless life on the run, however, begins to pall. Running of this kind (con man criminality) has only negative connotations, as he gradually realizes. Many of his old "running partners" are out of circulation, in prison, or "strung out" on drugs. He begins to feel a need for the kind of education he never bothered to get—school. The idea of going to school becomes a positive alternative to his life of crime, a way of escaping the treadmill trap into which his childhood running has led him. Claude Brown, like most runners who are driven by some inner necessity, is quick to move, to change place, to change role. Sonny has been a child terror, a delinquent, a thief, a liar; he metamorphoses into a pusher, a hustler, and finally a student. The new role is strange, one that he is unsure of. Only to himself does he admit the real reason he is going to school: "I wanted to get the hell out of Harlem. I needed a change and I started going for that reason" (Brown 1965, 201).

Leaving Harlem means leaving behind his fear and his gun. The symbol of manhood to Bigger Thomas and Dave ("Almos' a Man") is the opposite to Claude: "I gave my gun away when I moved out of Harlem. I felt free. This was one of the things that made me feel free, that I didn't need a gun, I didn't need any kind of protection, because I wasn't afraid any more" (Brown 1965, 193). Fear, from which Bigger was in constant flight, is an almost tangible reality of slum life. Every one of Sonny's running partners at one time or another is motivated by fear: fear of fighting or not fighting, of beatings by parents or total neglect, of starvation, of stealing and being caught or not stealing and failing to measure up to gang life, of getting "hooked" on drugs. Danny, one of the few to recover from heroin addiction, explains the connection between drugs and fear to Claude, who never becomes addicted because of an early terrifying experience with drugs:

[Junkies are] "just a bunch of little chumps, man, just the way I was, scared to live. Scared, that's all it is. You can't talk people out of fear, man. You just can't do it. You got to let them grow up and one day stop runnin'." (Brown 1965, 251)

Unlike Huck, whose flight was a positive alternative to society's evils, Danny chose a completely negative alternative—drugs. Taking drugs was a manifestation of fear, a way of running *from* life. Running for Danny was therefore self-destructive. Claude is only able to recognize the meaning of "the plague" (addiction) when he is away from the drug scene, in his No Man's Land between the Village and Harlem, when he is not completely a part of either. For him, running at this point is a positive reflex, an attempt to escape the gutter life of Harlem and the criminal identity to which he has been tied, but he does not divorce himself from black life. Harlem is still his "point of reference," but from a distance he is able to see things differently.

Brown does not run white nor does he run far, yet he is one of the most successful youthful runners at leaving behind his old identity. His running is ambiguous because it starts as an escape from his family's black peasant past; it becomes criminal activity because that is the way to identity "out in the streets." His next phase of running, however, is to escape that criminal identity; it is a quest for a mature sense of self and a move away from fear, "toward challenges, toward the positive anger" that he thinks every young man should have (Brown 1965, 414). When he returns to Harlem, he *is* running from the abuses of the white world, with the realization that he has a place of refuge, a community to which he can return: "I was hurt, and I was running home" (Brown 1965, 354).

Claude's recognition of Harlem as home, despite its being in part a political and social wasteland for his people, brings about an acceptance, not a rejection, of black reality. His running does not bring him full circle as it did Bigger; unlike the odysseys of Huck and Holden, Claude's travels lead him *back to* society. His attempt to redefine himself in relationship to a dynamic, complex yet changing black society is successful. He does not take Ras's way, or Rinehart's, the Coptics' or the Muslims'. He learns what he needs to know by seeing more—exploring the white community and white relationships, white jazz and black jazz. The double vision he gains by running, by being "out of it" for a time, becomes a way of seeing back into it with feeling and perception. Once he becomes secure in his new self-image he is, like the Invisible Man, reborn into the place of his birth: "It was as though I had found my place and Harlem had found its place. We were suited for each other now" (Brown 1965, 360).

The fact that *Manchild* is a "success" story, as Jarrett points out,[10] separates it philosophically from Richard Wright's autobiography. The social criticism, handled with honesty and a rare amount of objectivity, is, however, just as gripping an indictment of society's wanton disregard for its black citizens as is *Black Boy*. Sonny's experience as a runner, like Holden's and Huck's, becomes a criticism of American life. In his travels he exposes senseless brutality that makes the feud between the Grangerfords and the Shepherdsons look like a gentlemen's disagreement, viciousness that puts the Duke and the Dauphin to shame, and deprivation that makes Huck's life seem like a pastoral romance. The black experience in America, and especially in slum America, deprives its young of a portion of life—childhood. Reno's dissertation on the manchild gives added emphasis to the title of Brown's autobiography: "Man, Sonny, they ain't got no kids in Harlem. I ain't never seen any. I've seen some real small people actin' like kids, but they don't have no kids in Harlem, because nobody has time for a childhood" (Brown 1965, 285).

When "Saint Paul and the Monkeys" (*Dancers on the Shore,* 1964) opens, William Kelley's protagonist, Chig Dunford, is about the same age as Claude Brown at the close of *Manchild*. Chig, however, is the product of a comfortable home, the son of a successful *Negro* doctor in white Westchester county, light-years away from Claude's black Harlem. Nevertheless, they do have some things in common. Neither fulfills the expectations of his community: Chig is expected to become a successful lawyer while Claude is expected to die violently at an early age. Claude is a fugitive from the iron circle of failure in the ghetto, and Chig is a fugitive from the sham and pretense of bourgeois society in the suburbs.

"Saint Paul and the Monkeys" deals with the common problem of a young man in love with a girl who represents everything he finds inimical in society. Avis is a thoroughly proper young woman with a "Polynesian" complexion that is clear, beautiful, and copper-colored, and she loves Chig as long as he follows the pattern prescribed by her family and the group: proposal, marriage, law school, home, children. Yet he continues to delude himself about her until revelation is forced upon him, not by God, but by a series of events that almost shatter his mind:

He could not arrange all his different emotions, but one picture kept exploding in his mind—of a baby monkey he had once seen on television that shivered and whimpered in the corner of a wire cage, as lights flashed and the arms of a weird contrivance clawed and battered the air. The monkey had been part of a psychological experiment. Stress had destroyed its mind.[11]

Chig's conversion comes somewhat later. When he tries to talk with Avis about his reluctance to become a lawyer, it becomes clear to him that she is unable to abide change or indecision. When Chig alternates between his psychic role of monkey-under-stress and Saint Paul before he sees the light, Avis finds him totally incomprehensible—not as obtuse as he find her, however, when he tries to talk with her about "the greatest book ever," *Huckleberry Finn*. It is no accident that we begin to associate Chig Dunford with Huck Finn; both turn their backs on the good and moral people of the town. Avis has thoroughly assimilated white, middle-class values, but Chig has not and, like Huck, he decides to go to hell. His method is to run from his decision to go to law school and from his commitment to conformity. Although Chig's escape is much more circumscribed, he is at least free *not* to be what Avis's father is, a tall, lean black suit, with "perfectly rounded spectacles," the hair of a British diplomat, and ministerial hands: a man with all the question marks erased from his life.

Kelley is obviously familiar with the successful, suburban *Negro*. His story is especially interesting for its insight into the lack of distinction between white and black at this level of society, and for its emphasis on the youth who is basically a cerebral runner, but in whose flight is implicit those higher values of human worth that perceptive young people fear have become vestigial in today's success culture. Chig is, for example, much more self-aware than Harry Angstrom, who functions on an entirely different psychic level. Rabbit *feels* life, he never *thinks* it; he acts on animal impulse and then lives in a state of intermittent anxiety.[12] Chig also experiences anxiety: witness the recurring thought of the quavering monkey, caged, alone, and suffering from stress inflicted upon him by insensitive humans. He is able, however, to experience revelation, even when painful. His movement away from society is much more positive than that of the frightened Rabbit or of the rhapsodic Dean Moriarty of Kerouac's *On the Road*, both runners of a kind.

The world that Kelley presents in "Saint Paul and the Monkeys" is not one of clear choice. Avis is no termagant, nor is her father a villain.

Society is not as ugly or immoral as in the towns along the Mississippi, as schizophrenic as in Harry Angstrom's Pennsylvania town, or as repressive and prejudiced as in Kelley's own mythical southern state. It is the comfortable, cushioned existence of Westchester County, where everyone is something, where parents announce that their daughters are marrying a doctor or a lawyer, where mothers ask *what* he is, not *who* he is. In the final analysis, Chig objects to the lack of freedom, freedom to reject the mold, freedom to fail. Avis returns his ring in an obvious show of bravado. Because she never expects Chig to accept it, she is unable to contend with his strength. Although her position has been based on weakness, she expected to get what she wanted, as she always has, through threat or cajolery. When neither works, she faints—an old and learned feminine reaction. Chig's choice is to pick her up and get back into line, or leave her there; he chooses the latter. It is unchivalrous but honest and he feels himself again. What he wanted from Avis is what Erikson calls a "psychosocial moratorium," a delay of commitment, which she was unable to grant him.[13]

The experience of the young man going through an intense emotional crisis, a kind of initiation rite, is much like that of Mark Schorer's "Boy in the Summer Sun," in which the girl precipitates a crisis she cannot handle while the young man experiences both the pain and the growth. Kelley goes a step beyond the emotional crisis to make the point that those who belong to the establishment, whether black or white, are by virtue of their influence and affluence the arbiters of society, those who do the "sivilizing." In Chig's case, Avis is the instrument of the establishment, but she finds him as recalcitrant as Aunt Polly found Huck.[14]

Mance Bedlow of Kelley's "The Life You Save" (also from *Dancers on the Shore*) is one of those small people who have no time for childhood. His life is less closely analogous to Huck's, however, than it is to Bucky's, Danny's, or Reno's—Claude Brown's running partners. Kelley tells the story from the point of view of Peter, a college student working at a Harlem settlement house for the summer. Mance Bedlow is the most difficult boy in Peter's group of emotionally disturbed children. The director warns Peter:

"At eleven, this Mance Bedlow's seen it all. I can only tell you one thing: don't hit him, don't even try to punish him, or any of them. They've been smacked enough to last them a lifetime. That's why they're here. If you hit them, you'll lose them sure." (Kelley 1964, 144)

Peter is prepared and yet he isn't. Mance outwits him before the other boys with the ancient but effective substitute-teacher trick: he assumes another name and Peter foolishly tries to find Mance Bedlow while the other boys laugh at his gullibility. But when he looks into the boy's hard brown eyes, Peter realizes that at eleven, "he would not have survived in Mance Bedlow's world, even though he had always lived in Harlem. Peter's father was a doctor and earned a good living; Peter had been sent to private schools" (Kelley 1964, 147). When the boy becomes frustrated, he escapes to the street and Peter follows. Mance always threatens to go home but he never runs in that direction; he never runs *toward* anything:

Contrary to the declaration—"I'm going home!"—he never seemed to be heading toward any particular place. He simply ran until he got tired, or until Peter could engage him in conversation. Between flights he talked to no one. He would seem as engrossed as the other boys, then, suddenly, he would bolt." (Kelley 1964, 151-152)

Fear partially motivates the boy. He has no security in the streets except his own belligerence and no security at home where his physical safety is actually endangered. Violence is a part of Mance's family life as well as his street life. His "initiation rite" was actually and terribly by fire: his older brother tried to burn him alive and then attempted to "explain" his actions by saying that he was initiating Mance into a club. Mance's father, however, refused to believe that his namesake would do such a thing. Thus, he has no way of relating to the male figures in his family because his brother's sadistic perversion has alienated him from his father.

Mance has two alternatives to sustain his life: fight or flight. He is particularly accomplished as a runner (unlike Holden the prep-school fugitive, Mance's mobility is highly limited) but his course is circular; it begins and ends at the same place. The pity of childhood is that it is trapped by its own natural barriers. Even the terrible life of the slave seldom set the young child on the road. Frederick Douglass remained a slave for twenty-one years, as did William Wells Brown; the Crafts were married before they tried their daring escape; Josiah Henson was a slave for thirty-five or forty years. Only Gustavus Vassa, kidnaped at the age of eleven from his father's village, attempted to escape by running away. However, his kidnapers took him only as far as the next village, where he was enslaved by the chieftain. He had a place of security—his father's village—to escape to, and such an escape was in the realm of possibility. Mance Bedlow, on the other hand, is one of the boys in the promised land gone fallow, like Claude, Pimp, and Turk, but without Claude's intellectual resources. Mance has also been afflicted with psychological damage so that he is trapped in his own emotional cul-de-sac from which he cannot escape even by running. The Hudson River is not the Mississippi and the raft is out of date. Hence the car fixation: "When you get a car nobody can mess with you. . . . One of these days I'll hit the number and buy me a Cadillac and won't nobody mess with me" (Kelley 1964, 15). The Cadillac represents independence and manhood to the boy, as the gun does to Bigger and Dave, and, more important, it is the means to flight.

Mance can fight, of course. What he doesn't realize is that Peter can also fight when necessary. Through his own behavior, Peter has tried to show his eight charges that there is another way to survive, a way without violence and hate. But it is through his own fighting that the young counselor finally reaches them. When an older boy tries to intimidate them, Peter is so enraged that he cannot control his anger. The boys are shocked into speechlessness at the virulence of Peter's attack, while Mance looks on, scowling. When they return to the settlement house, Peter sends the boys home early and sits alone remonstrating with himself for having lost his temper, wondering how he can repair the damage he's done:

All summer, he had tried to build an image they could see and perhaps copy; he had tried to show them there were people in the world who were completely different from their aggressive, brutal fathers and brothers. In ten seconds, he had destroyed six weeks' work, and now he could not discover a way to salvage himself in their eyes. (Kelley 1964, 156)

Ironically, Mance now waits for Peter and follows him as Peter rushes for the bus. Mance wants to know if Peter learned to fight in college. Peter reluctantly admits that his father taught him to fight to protect himself. Mance is awed. Do doctors really fight? Peter is arrested by the boy's keen interest and the obvious admiration in his voice. He stares at Mance as the boy suddenly confesses, "When I was a kid I wanted to be a doctor" (Kelley 1964, 157).

Mance, like Huck, has "a profound and premature knowledge of human depravity,"[15] but unlike Huck, he has no ameliorating human experience. He is the symbol of a trapped and violated race. If Peter (here a fisher of boys) can save him, he can possibly save himself and his race. The ambiguity of Mance's (man's) flight is the ambiguity of the twentieth-century black Running Man: the need to escape the pain and ugliness of contemporary society before its crippling vise constricts his growth to that of a permanently dwarfed man-child. Yet, how does he cross over into manhood? Where is the newest Canaan? Kelley avoids sentimentalism and overt, awkward symbolism. The description of the boy's flight has none of the lyricism of Baraka's "Chase," but it is consistently and realistically handled. The dénouement is so aptly and simply expressed that the whole aborted life of a child devoid of hope is laid bare in one sentence—Mance Bedlow is all past and no future. Kelley may appear to be committed to finding a social role for Mance in this short story, but his attitude changes as he writes of this boy runner in his novel, *dem*. In that anti-integrationist work, Mance becomes a young Black Jesuit whose life is devoted to rebellion and revolt and whose time is dedicated to finding a way of annihilating whites.

Baraka's *Tales* (1967) is also separatist in mood. The first story in the book, entitled "A Chase (Alighieri's Dream)," written in the manner of his semi-autobiographical novel, *The System of Dante's Hell* (1965), is a brilliantly evocative tale of a youthful Running Man and his flight through the streets of Newark. Like Alan Sillitoe's long-distance runner, to whom loneliness is the "only honesty and realness there was in the world,"[16] the protagonist's lonely flight in space precipitates his flight of memory through time: "I was carrying groceries back across the manicured past."[17]

The story opens with a poetic, if disjointed, reminiscence of an unpoetic life, montage of a dream denied:

Place broken: their faces set and broke each other. As suns, Sons gone tired in the heart and left the south. The North, years later she'd wept for him drunk and a man finally they must have thought. In the dark, he was even darker. (Jones 1967, 1)

Here the history of the "Great Migration" is encapsulated, set down in Baraka's lean prose. His Newark, like Wright's Chicago and Claude Brown's Harlem, is the dead end of the promised land. The brevity of the language contrasts with the protracted frustration of the black sons who came North from the sunny South and are now broken, morally and physically, by the implacable hardness of the North itself, its unyielding coldness and ugliness, its lying promise: "Faces broke. Charts of age. Worn thru, to see black years. Bones in iron faces. Steel bones. Cages of decay." (Jones 1967, 1)

The nightmare, Baraka's Dantesque dream from which the runner flees, is the American inferno-city, with its symbols of death and decay. Like Rabbit Angstrom, the protagonist enjoys the exhilaration of running, the feel of escape, only this time it is escape from the depths. The hero, as Robert Bone points out, "becomes a broken-field runner, twisting past all that to some tremendous victory."[18] The broken-field runner is even more alone than the man on the basketball court. Already past the line of scrimmage, he has to overcome all the obstacles himself, with no protection from blockers:

Then only one man coming from the side . . . it went thru my head a million times, the years it took, seeing him there, with a good angle, shooting in, with 3 yards to the sidelines, about 10 home. I watched him all my life close it, and thot to cut, stop or bear down and pray I had speed. Answers shot up, but my head was full of blood and it moved me without talk. I stopped still the ball held almost like a basketball, wheeled and moved in to score untouched. (Jones 1967, 3)

The boy runs past scenes of drugs, gambling, homosexuality, violence, and thoughts of his own life of petty thievery, like Bigger's, but with this change: whites are now victims of *purposeful* revenge. "Up one block, crooked old Jews die softly under the moon. Past them. Past them. Their tombs and bones. Wet dollars blown against the fence" (Jones 1967, 2). The runner is victorious. He gains the heights by burning his way up the hill, and reaches an eminence where four corners come together, like the four corners of the earth: "4 corners, the entire world visible from there. Even to the lower regions" (Jones 1967, 4). From this point even the lower regions are visible, for the North is the ninth circle of hell where betrayers of their own kind are plunged into ice. One escapes or is forever held in frozen bondage.

The finale is a fine contrast to the opening word play, "son-sun." This runner has no guide. The most solitary of runners, he is more alone than Huck. It is Sunday when he emerges from the depths, but not Easter Sunday, for this is a secular dream. We know the day because the dream began on Saturday, and the runner has run the nightmare through, emerging in black wool: "Change clothes on the street to a black suit. Black wool" (Jones 1967, 4). Black is the color for victory.

Though only four pages long, "A Chase" is extraordinarily dense and allusive. None of the younger black writers has Baraka's skill with words and images. Baraka's youthful runner is filled with pain and confusion. Completely alienated, he intends to make it out of the stereotyped depths into a separateness of his own choosing, an identity of his own making. Baraka continues to dramatize his aggressive negritude in prose, poetry, and especially in the theater, addressing his *black* drama to *black* audiences. His aesthetic dictum was pronounced in "The Revolutionary Theater," an essay first published in the *Liberator* in 1965. Black theater is revolutionary and must move to action; it must be a viable force for change. "It must move to reshape the world."

This is a theater of assault. The play that will split the heavens for us will be called THE DESTRUCTION OF AMERICA. The heroes will be Crazy Horse, Denmark Vesey, Patrice Lumumba, and not history, not memory, not sad sentimental groping for a warmth in our despair; these will be new men, new heroes, and their enemies most of you who are reading this. [19]

Baraka, too, is a runner of a sort, with protean guises of his own.

Harold Cruse remarks that his personal misgivings about Baraka grew out of his critical responses to Baraka's different poses and postures:

As it turns out these [Barakan] posturings have not been all upstage antics but rather the ambivalence of the the supreme actor brazenly in search of just the right "role" that would best suit the purpose in life of the real man inside [Baraka].[20]

Imamu Amiri Baraka seems to be the right role for the political-revolutionary-artist, and for him apparently it is the fire *this* time.

NOTES

1. From Robert Coles's interview with a black child in "It's the Same, but It's Different," *The Negro American*, ed. Talcott Parsons and Kenneth B. Clark (Boston, 1966), p. 258.
2. I am indebted for this synthesis to Charles Kaplan for his excellent discussion of Huck and Holden as youthful travelers in "Holden and Huck: The Odysseys of Youth," *College English* XVIII (November 1956): 76-80.
3. Ibid., p. 78.
4. The youthful runner has received publicity in the Detroit press. In an article on the 12th Street Academy, a storefront school opened by the Urban League on the site of one of the country's worst riots, Helen Fogel, the staff writer, explains that the school's purpose is "to gather in the boy who's 'running' on 12th." (*Detroit Free Press*, November 17, 1968, p. 1C.)
5. Kaplan, *Holden and Huck*, p. 77.
6. Hobart Jarrett, "Review," *Phylon* XXVII (1956): 206.
7. Claude Brown, *Manchild in the Promised Land* (New York, 1965) p. 7.
8. Maya Angelou's "Daddy Clidell" *wanted* her to be educated in the con game so that she would never be "anybody's mark." Her teachers were "Stonewall Jimmy, Just Black, Cool Clyde, Tight Coat and Red Leg . . . the most successful con men in the world," all from the "Black Underground" of San Francisco. They took turns showing her their tricks, "how they chose their victims (marks) from the wealthy bigoted whites and in every case how they used their victims' prejudice against them." (*I Know Why the Caged Bird Sings* [New York, 1970], p. 187.)
9. Con men figure prominently in the detective novels of Chester Himes, but as objects of disesteem. They are prime targets of Grave Digger Jones and Coffin Ed Johnson, two black detectives who have their own interpretation of law enforcement: "Some people they never touched—such as madams of orderly houses of prostitution, operators of orderly gambling games, . . . street-walkers who stayed in their district. But they were rough on criminals of violence and confidence men." (*The Big Gold Dream* [New York, 1966], p. 62; originally published in France as *Tout pour Plaire*, 1960.)
10. Jarret, "Review," p. 206.
11. William Melvin Kelley, *Dancers on the Shore* (Garden City, New York, 1964), p. 69. Further citations will be in the text.
12. Rabbit's reaction follows its own pattern: pass the ball when there are too many

on you: "So you passed and the ball belonged to the others and your hands were empty and the men on you looked foolish because in effect there was nobody there." (John Updike, *Rabbit Run* [New York, 1960], p. 306.) Rabbit's running is an escape from home and family (although he does "return home" in *Rabbit Redux*, New York, 1971). He is another American male with the ingenuous charm of youth, but he is beyond the Huck Finn-Holden Caulfield age of innocence so that the handsome, carefree sprinter-lover has a self-conscious quality, the strange odor of youth preserved too long, like the heavy smell of Neet's Foot oil in the thongs of a baseball glove.

13. Erik H. Erikson, *Identity: Youth and Crisis* (New York, 1968), p. 156.

14. Kelley's latest novel, *Dunfords Travels Everywheres* (1970) is, in a "langleash" of its own, a continuation of Chig Dunford's life. Now a writer-on-the-road, Chig is not only a traveler abroad (Kelley has created a mythical European country this time, populated by Atzuoreurso and Jualoreurso natives as well as ubiquitous, touring Americans) but also a traveler on several planes of consciousness, on a journey toward self-discovery. Carlyle Bedlow (of *dem*) makes his appearance as a Cooley Johnson type of con man. He and Chig are the Harlem black and the Harvard black, as Michael Wood says in his review of the novel, "aspects, ultimately, of a single self [who] meet on the common ground of their color and their alienation." (*New York Review of Books*, March 11, 1971, p. 43)

15. David Galloway, *The Absurd Hero in American Fiction* (Austin, Texas, 1966), p. 94.

16. Alan Sillitoe, *The Loneliness of the Long-Distance Runner* (New York, 1960), p. 43.

17. LeRoi Jones, *Tales* (New York, 1967), p. 1. Further citations will be in the text.

18. Robert Bone, "De Profundis," The *New York Times*, February 4, 1968, Sec. 7, p. 36.

19. LeRoi Jones, "The Revolutionary Theater," *Liberator* 5, no. 7 (July 1965): 14.

20. Harold R. Cruse, *The Crisis of the Negro Intellectual* (New York, 1967), p. 538.

8. THE BLACK RUNNER AS CONFIDENCE MAN

"Modern life is a kind of confidence game."
Richard Wright, *The Outsider*

Two novels published in 1967 deal with the Running Man symbol in uniquely different ways. Kelley's *dem* reflects both the influence of Rinehartism (Ellison's "confidencing sonofabitch") and the folklore "trickster." John A. Williams's *The Man Who Cried I Am* develops that relatively new fictional character, the black espionage agent, who stems from Richard Wright's and perhaps his own experiences as expatriate writer abroad. Always an intransigent, Wright was unwilling to play either the East or the West game in the Cold War European arena and for this reason was apparently kept under surveillance by assorted CIA agents. The black agent surprised yet fascinated him:

it was, or appeared to be, a fairly simple conviction: Negroes were human beings. But he knew it was a shattering concept when pursued to the end. The proof had shocked even Richard: black men could be as corrupt as white men. They could be, quite possibly, even more corrupt in some situations, if he followed out another thesis of his—that the Negro was also special, advanced and gifted with double vision.[1]

That double vision, as we have seen, has been characterisitc of the Running Man, allowing him to function both outside and inside society at the same time. For an espionage agent, it is an essential attribute, and Wright recognized that the role of spy[2] was made to order for the Afro-American:

As an outsider he has always looked on and observed, which has given him a keen sensitivity toward the functioning of the mind and personality of the oppressor. Diplomacy is not something he has to learn; all his life he have lived by subterfuge, masking his face, ferreting out information, merely to survive. As a child he has learned to watch the faces of white people on whom he was dependent to see if they would kick him, kill him or pat him on the head and give him a quarter. Thus, the faintest twitch of a lip, a shadow across the eyes, or no expression at all is a Morse code he knows how to read. His entire life has been, in a sense, a spying on white America. In Paris, spying, as conducted by white men, is literally child's play to a black man:[3]

Williams has caught the black confidence man abroad in *The Man Who Cried I Am*. The story is told from the point of view of Max Reddick, Williams's persona, a black writer, occasional expatriate, and friend of Harry Ames, the fairly obvious fictional counterpart of Richard Wright. Indeed the entire book is a hunting ground for familiar faces. There are a Malcolm X (Minister Q) who is gunned down at a meeting, a James Baldwin (Marion Dawes) who attacks Harry in essay form, an Ellison, a James Meredith, a southern civil rights leader, and even a young American President. The Wright character is most easily identifiable. Harry Ames is an expatriate runner, born in Mississippi, who has moved on to Chicago and New York before leaving the United States for France. A disaffected former member of the Communist Party and an outspoken and embittered writer, he travels to Africa and Asia writing provocative essays on social, economic, and political topics. America's foremost black author, he becomes a part of the French existentialist coterie for a time, and later is refused a visa to live in England. Williams adds numerous fictional (and sexual) embellishments to each of his originals, but the essential problem of intrigue has its basis in the reality of black expatriate life.

Both Harry Ames and Max Reddick are killed by Alphonse Edwards, a black CIA agent, with the assistance of Roger Wilkinson, his partner. Ames and Reddick have to be eliminated because they both learn about "King Alfred," the United States government's genocide plan to eliminate its black minority. The black espionage agent is a different breed of Running Man and a special breed of con man, born of the band of expatriate Americans in Europe who, as T. J. Fleming points out, "ultimately find themselves ciphers, men without a country."[4] Harry and Max are runners we have seen before: outsiders, strongly independent and talented individuals, blacks who refuse to stand still with their anger. But Edwards and Roger Wilkinson are of the group Wright described at the American Church of Paris, explaining to his audience, with some ironic humor, that the black spy's job was difficult, that all people dislike spies, but that the black spy should be viewed with some degree of compassion. For, social stratification being what it is in the ghetto, as in the black expatriate communities in Europe, it is "almost impossible for a black spy to fool his black brothers"[5] —his affluence is immediately suspect. For example, all spies must have a "cover story," but it is extremely difficult for black spies to fashion convincing cover identities.

Williams's CIA agents, however, have developed extraordinarily sophisticated "covers." Edwards and Roger Wilkinson, the two most important black spies in *The Man Who Cried I Am*, are totally different expatriate types, yet they play their roles so convincingly that Harry never suspects either. Harry's closest contact is with Edwards, whom Max describes as:

a black Ivy Leaguer. Close-cropped hair, for he *wanted* Europeans to know that he was American. The other Negroes let their hair grow long and bushy—nappy—in order to be mistaken for Africans. Not Edwards. American all the way. Red white and black.[6]

Max has already met Edwards briefly at a party in Lagos, when he was on assignment in Africa for *Pace*, an American news magazine. At the time Edwards was a political affairs officer, the newest *Negro* addition to the American Embassy, but Max was not drawn to the type:

Edwards was a good mixer, tall, cool, with an intelligent bright face, definitely American. . . . He slid without pause from the stilted conversational style of government man with many secrets, to the vernacular of the bar at the Red Rooster in Harlem. (Williams 1967, 329)

Actually, Edwards appears sparingly in the novel; he is usually seen out of the corner of someone's eye. Max sees him next at Harry's funeral; Edwards arrives in Amsterdam "coincidentally" when Max meets Margrit, his estranged Dutch wife, the following day; and Max sees him for the last time on the wrong side of a gun. Until the funeral, Max has only a sense of discomfort in Edwards's presence, although "he has *not* liked Edwards from the first, from Nigeria. Even less since he had been with Harry when Harry died" (Williams 1967, 12). Max isn't satisfied with Edwards's story of Harry's death:

He and Harry were walking out of the Rue de Berri and paused at the corner waiting for a traffic light to change. Harry had gone down. . . . "Boom, like that." Edwards had said in Paris, his lean face suggesting rather than actually possessing sorrow. Max remembered that even then he wondered just why Harry would bother with a type like that. He must have been getting senile. (Williams 1967, 12-13)

Edwards's story apparently satisfies everyone else, although Max knows or thinks he knows that Harry would never die "Boom, like that....Why not? ... Because he was too goddammed evil" (Williams 1967, 13).

Roger Wilkinson is, of course, Max's blind spot. He never suspects Roger just as Harry never suspects Edwards. In fact, Max visits Wilkinson, who is now living in Amsterdam, to ask about Edwards:

"That cat! ... I see him around when he's in town. That's about all. I guess he writes. I've heard he writes. He loads up a car with articles and drives around Europe selling them to papers and magazines. You know, crap all prepared, and about half of it plagiarized. I mean, these people over here just don't know." (Williams 1967, 27)

Max is still suspicious and he asks Roger directly whether Edwards is a fink. "A Fink. No, man.... If the government planted a fink, wouldn't they make him to be one of the boys, you know, not sharp, an artist, starving" (Williams 1967, 27). And he goes on to describe himself. It is a shrewd maneuver and it works. "Now, Edwards, he's just a little bit away from everybody. Uncle Sam don't work that way. In the middle, right down the middle" (Williams 1967, 27).

The contrast between Edwards and Wilkinson is extreme. We never know much more about Edwards, except that he has been involved in Alliance Blanc, a white international conspiracy to subvert African independence, in Africa and Europe. Harry's last letter to Max is proof of how well Edwards's cover identity has worked:

Another item, old buddy. Tomorrow I'm having lunch with a young man I understand you've met. His name is Edwards, and he's quit Uncle Sam's foreign service to write a novel about it. I can't resist these youngsters who come to see me, to sit at the feet of the father, so to speak. I guess I'll never outgrow it. I suppose you're next in line to be father....(Williams 1967, 370)

Harry's pride and vanity help to conceal the truth from him, just as Max's intolerance and indifference help to conceal the truth about Roger.

Roger Wilkinson is an acquaintance, if not a friend, of long standing. Max had known him and his father back in the States. "Then Roger had come to Europe. To be free" (Williams 1967, 26). Unlike Edwards, Wilkinson is on speaking terms with the black expatriate community in France, in Holland, wherever the blacks in foreign countries cluster together, even though he is always on the run:

He'd always left his places of residence a mystery. "I'm into my thing," he would explain, and vanish, and in Europe, the black artists went along with your wish to be left alone, most of the time. Until you started to make it, then they came back to bug you into failure. (Williams 1967, 26)

They don't have to do this with Roger because he is a portrait of the artist as failure. Having written three novels and sold none, he has only one method of staying alive other than doing instant articles on race riots for foreign papers—women. Roger is what Max calls a "macker," but not an ordinary one. He "gave a little more than most Negroes in Europe who were thus engaged between books or articles or showings or jazz engagements." Roger gave his women "laughs and little peeks" at black and white culture through the ages. "Roger macked with finesse" (Williams, 1967, 18).

Max cannot tolerate Roger's inability to face the reality that he is *not* a writer. Roger's father knows, yet he sends money to his son via Max in spite of his own illness: "He thinks you're pretending; he thinks you're afraid to go home and take your lumps with the rest of the spades" (Williams 1967, 30). Roger won't discuss his father except as a giver of alms, and he plays his role of hungry, alienated artist to the full—at what point he changes into his agent's role is not made explicit. Max is aware, however, that the suffering writer mask is a pretense: "As a Negro, he [Roger] hadn't suffered, hadn't armied in the South, hadn't been hungry, and he had never gone south of Manhattan. Roger's Negro anger was ersatz; ersatz, but useful. If he hadn't been Negro, he would have no reason on earth to raise his voice, or want to write" (Williams 1967, 29). In fact, Roger has always done more talking than writing, and he always gave the impression that he knew exactly what he was doing.

For no apparent reason, Max recalls various things about Roger as his last day moves to a close. Roger was always a name dropper, not just all the books he had read but all the places he had been, "including a Catholic college that specializes in prelaw courses and which was always being visited by the FBI and CIA to recruit personnel from among the student body. 'Man, they talked to me, once'" (Williams 1967, 191). There had been laughter at the thought that the CIA would bother with a clown like Roger. Then there was Roger's ubiquity. Max remembered how he was always turning up in Paris, laughing over coffee; in Rome on the Via Veneto talking Italian to the hippies; sauntering down the Leidsestraat; Roger everywhere. He had met Max at Orly when Max was doing an article on expatriates for *Pace*; he was with Margrit when Max returned to Amsterdam from Africa. He is also linked in Max's mind with Ted Dallas (a minor character but a major agent in the hierarchy), both of whom have a knack for doing and saying "everything at just the right time and the right place" (Williams 1967, 259). The fact remains that with all of Max's retrospective insight, he is surprised to death by both Alphonse Edwards and Roger Wikinson.

The question of motivation looms large for the three black espionage agents, and Williams does not entirely answer it. Ted Dallas, with whom we have the least concern because he is not, strictly speaking, a Running Man, is apparently motivated by political ambition and by some distorted sense of social responsibility. He is amazed, for example, that Harry and Max would think of "trying to wreck the country as they could with the information about Alliance Blanc. All the little people they said they cared about in their writing, would be the first to go" (Williams 1967, 393). He is much more amazed when he discovers the existence and the meaning of King Alfred, and realizes that he and the little people are expendable. Roger Wilkinson, on the other hand, is obviously money motivated. He has graduated from conning his father to conning his friends and acquaintances on an international level. But Alphonse Edwards is as "red white and black" as Max had originally thought. He sees himself in the role of protector of Americans too puerile to protect themselves, and he carries out his role with equanimity:

The new assignment would be another of what the people back home called dirty, filthy jobs. But those jobs protected America in ways Americans were too childish to realize. However, they did expect someone to protect them. From all terrors. (Williams 1967, 396)

What neither Edwards nor Wilkinson realizes is how far they themselves have been conned. As operators on the international scale, they differ from petty street con men like Rinehart in *Invisible Man* and Johnny D in *Manchild in the Promised Land.* Those small-time operators, however, knew the territory; they were never the dupes of their own game.

Ironically, Harry Ames also turns out to be a confidence man. Max finally sees the man behind the mask. For Williams is writing about con men white and black; his book is peopled with them, from office boy to president, and Max Reddick, his persona, has Melville on the mind:

He wanted to do with the novel what Charlie Parker was doing to music— tearing it up and remaking it; basing it on nasty, nasty blues and overlaying it with the deep overriding tragedy not of Dostoevsky, but an American who knew of consequences to come: Herman Melville, a super Confidence Man, a Benito Cereno saddened beyond death. (Williams 1967, 209)

Confidence is a metaphor of corrupt man in *The Man Who Cried I Am,* and the epitome of corrupt man is the black espionage agent, cunningly recruited from the ranks of expatriate runners. But Harry surpasses the bland corruption of the paid agent. Out of jealousy of Max, the black writer next in line for his "crown" and the one man he would hate most for displacing him even momentarily with his wife, he decides that Max is the one to get the King Alfred information. Apparently willing to sacrifice Michelle, the woman he loves, to get revenge, Harry cons her into giving Max the papers that will lead to their certain death:

It was that, huh, Harry, that and the books, huh, baby? The writing, the White House, and all the time you were getting tired and weak and bitter. All the things you thought I had, you should have had, being Harry Ames. Man, I know how that can be. This revenge is worthy of you. But—anything to get even with me? Even Michelle? Jesus. But do you know what you've done, finally, *finally*? You've shared with me! Now your generosity is supposed to kill me. . . .This is the jungle side, then, thick with years of pretense and so normal in appearance! This is where the crawling things are, in this place and all around us. (Williams 1967, 379)

Williams's universe is as godless as Melville's and man—"Man is nature, nature man, and all crude and raw, stinking, vicious, evil (Williams 1967, 377).

The White Alliance to subvert African independence and the King Alfred plan to eliminate America's black minority is the recurring nightmare of Williams's tormented world. In that world the theme of betrayal of brother by brother is ironically and compellingly revealed: "Before the black VW had stopped, Max recognized Roger and Edwards, and thought without surprise, Of course! . . .This is the final irony. The coming of age, Negro set at Negro in the name of God and country" (Williams 1967, 400-401).

Ed Bullins's protagonist in *The Reluctant Rapist*, a novel published some six years after *The Man Who Cried I Am*, contains a similar revelation, although it does not lead to imminent death:

The world prepares the black man in a single skill: treachery to his fellows.

No man lies to a black man more than another black man. No man cheats or is as ready to kill another black man as is another black man. One must become accustomed to the perplexities of this brotherhood and learn and understand why. One must lose faith, for faith is never quite enough. One must throw away belief, for belief is held by every black fool. One must be blown apart by all that one has been taught and reassembled in the vacuum of ignorance to form the vessel of new experience.

There is not a white man alone I fear to face, though I am wary of each of my black brothers, for ancient betrayal waits behind each smile and set of dark eyes.[7]

Running black con men in fiction do not always dupe or betray their own; some, in fact, by reversing the roles of victim and victimizer, bring about a new sense of solidarity in the black community . Although Cooley Johnson, the running confidence man in Kelley's *dem*, is not the novel's central figure, his shifting presence is essential to the plot. He is the elusive character Mitchell Pierce must find, the key to Mitchell's future. Calvin Coolidge Johnson, however, is another black man who refuses to stand still for the whites. His running, inspired by white racism, is negative from a white's point of view but positive for the blacks. Less an escape than a subtle, aggressive posture, Cooley's actions produce the turmoil and conflict in *dem*, which is told from the point of view of Mitchell Pierce, a white advertising writer. Kelley's Running Man is developed from the rich materials of the black antebellum past, as well as from the con man tradition of white American literature. When Cooley confronts Mitchell, he first assumes the guise of the folklore trickster; finally he becomes the avenger on the run. Their confrontation has the ring of history.

Kelley's attack is leveled at the northern white middle class, geographically urban, emotionally infantile. He sets his "average" New York couple, Tam and Mitchell Pierce, into a bizarre conflict with the Harlem subculture. For Tam, retaliating against Mitchell for his infidelity, takes a black lover. Neither intends for the other to find out, but Tam gives birth to twin boys—one white, one black. Kelley says in his phonetic subtitle: "Now, lemme tell ya how dem folks live."

The role of the blacks is kept carefully in the background until the birth of the babies, then the book's emphasis quickly changes. For our purposes the most important section is "Twins," in which Kelley is again the fabulist of *A Different Drummer*. He asks the reader to accept, as do Swift and most satirists, one major assumption, and from this the conclusion is developed logically and consistently. In *A Different Drummer* it was that there exists in the United States one exclusively white southern state. In *dem* the one rather large assumption is documented in a note prefixed to the novel:

Superfecundation is the fertilization of two ova within a short period of time by spermatozoa from separate copulations. It is only distinguishable from usual two-egg twinning if the female has coitus with two males with diverse physical characters, each passing his respective traits to the particular twin he has fathered.

—Alan F. Guttmacher, *Pregnancy and Birth.*[8]

When Tam gives birth to fraternal twins, the doctor, unable to explain the extraordinary event to Mitchell, leaves him unenlightened at the nursery window. Confused by a Cuban father who claims one of the white babies as his own, Mitchell makes the painful discovery that "El negrito, as the Cuban called it [is] named Pierce" (Kelley 1967, 126).

Tam is not contrite. She tells Mitchell that Cooley is the baby's father, but that the whole affair is Mitchell's fault—he drove her to it. A tenuous reconciliation is effected in the hospital bed as Tam kisses Mitchell on top of his boyish head while we are treated to the obvious symbolism of black needles and pink yarn. "Between her thighs the black needles stuck up out of the ball of pink wool" (Kelley 1967, 135). Although Tam wants to keep the black baby to remind Mitchell of their past unhappiness, Tam's mother, a domineering and aging seductress, wants Mitchell to get rid of the baby and reestablish the marriage. She manipulates him—Tam and her mother are genuine Philip Wylie MOMS—into searching for the black baby's father and then leaves him a note congratulating him on his ability to make a decision.

Mitchell's only entrée to Cooley is Opal Simmons, the black maid he dismissed earlier in a racist frenzy. On his way to her apartment in the Bronx, he gradually becomes acquainted with a strange and threatening black world. He is confronted by a group of little girls jumping rope to the recitative of a symbolic slave song:

> Sitting in a teepee, smoking a pipe.
> Polar bear come with a great big knife.
> Polar bear take and put us in a boat.[9]
> So many children, thing couldn't float.
> Singing in a boat, with a necklace of iron.
> Bear come down and say, "You're mine."
> Children start crying, raise up a noise.
> Everybody's crying, even the boys. (Kelley 1967, 156-157)

Mitchell feels unsafe even among black children and not much more secure with a private black guard who tries to "protect" him.

Compliant Opal sends Mitchell to her nephew Carlyle, through whom she met Cooley. Carlyle listens to Mitchell's story and, evidently satisfied that he is not in any way official, proceeds ostensibly to help in the quest for Cooley. The first stop is a rent party where Carlyle passes Mitchell off as a Canadian cousin and introduces him to Calvin Johnson, supposedly a friend of Cooley's. From this point on Mitchell, who doesn't recognize Calvin, becomes the butt of the black world's joke. Calvin, with his shape-shifting skill, steps into the classic role of the clever *eiron*, while Mitchell becomes his victim, the hypocritical *alazon* completely lacking in self-knowledge. Although he is yet unaware of the process, Mitchell's education has begun. None of the people he now encounters thinks white or wishes to be part of or to emulate white society. In fact, the color itself is anathema to them. Mitchell understands this as little as he does the folkways and the argot of the black community.

After a kind of surreal Nighttown scene, Mitchell finds himself bedded down with Glora, a friend of Carlyle's, whose help he seeks in his quest for Cooley. However, Glora doesn't react as he predicted, even when he finally tells her that his wife has had Cooley's baby. She says that Cooley will not take the baby but Mitchell doesn't believe her. The evening ends unsatisfactorily, sexually and otherwise, for Mitchell, and he hallucinates his way through the rest of the night, awakening only to the news from Tam's mother that his baby is dead.

Kelley has sprinkled enough clues throughout the last section to make clear that Cooley and Calvin Johnson are the same person. With the right touch of dramatic irony, Kelley allows his character to learn too late all he is ever to know from the man for whom he is searching. Calvin brings a message from Cooley who still chooses to remain "invisible." Mitchell, however, is convinced that money will bring Cooley out of hiding, and he forces $70 on Calvin before the icy awareness sets in. Not only has he been "had" but so has his wife, and Mitchell is left holding the baby.

Calvin Coolidge Johnson is the Running Man as confidence man, an outsider who doesn't want in. He functions on the edge of the law and is protected by the blacks who admire and respect him. He is blood brother to the familiar "trickster" of Afro-American folklore, whose name was usually Jack or John; here it is John-son. As "Calvin" Johnson, Cooley plays the good and moral Christian, appearing to assist his white "brother." The "Calvin Coolidge" tag is the added freight that Cooley (the "Cool Man") carries, a satiric thrust at the tradition that once produced so many black George Washingtons.[10] In slavery the trickster

had a made-to-order setting. Surprised in his folly or his wrong-doing by Old Master, Old Miss, the "patterollers," or even the devil, he would attempt to clear himself by his wit. He did not always succeed, but the happy ending was when he avoided a whipping or, better still, obtained his freedom. In the course of the tales the storytellers poked as much fun at themselves as they did at their masters, but pretentiousness was unfailingly exposed.[11]

"Polite" white society has no attraction for Cooley, although he was willing to view it at close range when the opportunity presented itself:

"Your wife? He saw her and wanted to find out how someone that evil and messed up in the head would be in bed. It was so bad, and weak, he had to go back a couple of times to make sure it was really as bad as he thought it was the first time." (Kelley 1967, 203)

Cooley's next opportunity comes when Mitchell tries to extricate himself and Tam from any responsibility for the black baby. This is Cooley's chance to avenge his people for years of slaveholding wrongs:

"Old scores from four hundred years ago, for his great-grandaddy and his grandaddy. That's another thing about Cooley. He is a grudge-holding Black man. He don't never forget a slight. Like what old scores? Like having a wife or a girl you really love and then she gets big with a baby, and you happy as a champ. But when the baby comes, God damn, it ain't yours. You can't blame your woman; she a slave too. And you can't do nothing about it yourself. So you just eat shit, and you and your woman take and raise that kid. Then one day, after you and the baby get good and attached, its natural father up and sells it away from you. So you lost a kid, but you never really had one. So he says, it's your turn." (Kelley 1967, 204)

This paragraph contains the essence of pain found in countless slave narratives. Relationships between men and women slaves were tenuous at best. Marriages were easily dissolved and remade for the convenience of the master—slaves did not have the power to enter into such contractual arrangements. In fact, as Charles Nichols points out, "Legal marriages would have been an offense not only to the owner's economic interest but also to his licentious appetite. For in the breeding of slaves many masters and overseers were their own studs."[12]

dem reverses the roles; the "stud" is black and neither slave nor servant. In effect, Cooley is saying, "Let's see how you like it." When Mitchell asks, "But why me?" Cooley replies with the logic of black experience, "Why my great-grandaddy?" Cooley, the avenger on the run, slips in and out of the Pierces's sick little ménage with equanimity. He and his friends, completely disabused of the romantic notion of equality and integration, have settled down to divorce, alienation, and disaffection from the white community. Theirs is a separate but superior existence, if not in affluence, certainly in a newfound sense of community and self-esteem. Their group morality is based on a negatively structured counterpart of the dominant white culture. What is legal in the white courts is, ipso facto, taboo in Cooley Johnson's practical world; what is acceptable behavior for "Sir Charles the White Knight" is by definition egregious, repugnant, and ludicrous. White is evil (devil), black is good and beautiful. The sentiments are much like those of Ras the Exhorter, but the approach is far more subtle, and the methods are tactically similar to those of Jim Crow—psychological destruction. For Mitchell is attacked in the solar plexus of his manhood. Not only is his wife an obvious adulteress but Mitchell is unmanned by the quest. The age-old Telemachian search for identity through a father image is changed to the search for a father (brother), which ironically ends in total rejection. Cooley is a "honky-hater" in the new tradition with a secure identity in his own viable underground community. Mitchell, on the other hand, has lost both his identity and his masculinity. His only hope was to find Cooley and through him to find himself.

Bone feels that "with his central image of the twins, Kelley reminds us that white and black Americans are virtually brothers, that denial of fraternity is our historic crime."[13] Actually, Kelley is reminding us that our historic crime has already been committed, with the result that the black man has now accepted that denial and wants, in fact *demands*, freedom *from* fraternity. The use of Tam as a tool and the rejection of Mitchell as co-genitor and thus brother are both expedients to the destruction of the white image, the Old South's method in reverse. And the *coup de grace* is that Mitchell's child is the one that "just died"; the strong child is the black one, the child he is at last forced to father. This is as unusual in our literature as the Indian surviving the white man, so unusual in fact that Fiedler discusses in great detail the one book (Kesey's *One Flew Over the Cuckoo's Nest*) in which the "colored"—the Indian, in this case—partner outlives his white brother:

Typically, Chingachgook has predeceased Natty, and Queequeg, Ishmael; typically, Huck had been younger than Jim, Ike than Sam Fathers. Everyone who has lived at the heart of our dearest myth knows that it is the white boy-man who survives.[14]

Evidently Kelley no longer accepts our dearest myth; perhaps he is creating one of his own.[15]

Most of the characters in *dem* are essentially caricatures: Tam, the selfish bitch; Opal, the honest domestic; Cooley, the flashy "nigger." Mitchell is a kind of Thurber-cartoon male swallowed whole by the female. He is so nominally successful in his own world that it is hardly surprising to see him blunder about in a world he considers both alien and sinister. He suffers from the gross prejudices: "All blacks look alike; they'll do anything for money; they're stupid, dishonest and thieving; they all want to be white." His lack of perception makes him a perfect foil for Cooley, who, in spite of his marginal existence, is a man, revenging his male antecedents.

Kelley is clearly in touch with the shifting realities of Afro-American life in the late sixties. There is no passive resistance in these northern black urbanites who fight together for economic and emotional survival. Without hesitation they have identified the common enemy: Whitey, Mister Charlie, Honky. Whether all whites are bad is no longer a pertinent question; stereotypes are just as useful to the oppressed as they have always been to the oppressor. Some landlords are Jews; therefore, all Jews are slumlords, and when Kelley's blacks cannot pay the rent, they have rent parties "to pay the Jew." Claude Brown uses a similar stereotype when he mentions that the women who came to "the promised land" ended up scrubbing "Goldberg's" floors. The women at the party are convinced that "cousin" Mitchell is not all man because he has lived too long among whites and integration means psychic castration. Glora tells him that he needs a couple of drinks: "That's the way the white folks do, ain't it? Can't have a good time until they get drunk and start breaking things. . . . Sometimes I think the Jesuits is right. I seen more good niggers get ruined by integration!" (Kelley 1967, 176). Separation is the only route to survival.

Although Kelley offers no answers, he does hold the reality of long years of separation, in mirror image, up to the American mind. He also emphasizes the extent of that separateness by dedicating his novel to "The Black people in (not of) America," a sentiment that echoes Richard Wright's "Outsider," who "sensed how Negroes had been made to live in but not of the land of their birth."[16] The satire is sure, sharp, and extraordinarily well aimed.

The spirit in which Kelley wrote *dem* seems closely akin to that in which Melville wrote *The Confidence Man*. Certainly the satire arises from the changeless times the black man has experienced in America. Kelley's first novel, *A Different Drummer*, exuded some of the confidence of the early civil rights struggle. However, by 1967, some one hundred years after Melville's loss of confidence in the moral order of the universe, it was clear that an entente with the white community, based on a genuine change in the economic and social position of blacks in America, was as unlikely in this century as voluntary manumission of all slaves was in the last. Both *dem* and *The Confidence Man* appear to be products of disaffected writers in disenchanted times. Newton Arvin's assumption that Melville was losing "for the moment his last shred of confidence in both nature and man"[17] seems reasonable, and it seems abundantly clear that Kelley has no confidence in either nature *or* the white man. The difference is that Kelley has not lost his confidence in black men. In fact, the black confidence man in *dem* becomes a kind of folk hero.

Strongly emphasized in *dem* is the emptiness and moral decay of the white world. In *The Confidence Man*, Melville emphasizes the metaphysical emptiness of the entire universe. Kelley's fictional design, in contrast, is reduced and particularized. His is not a world of fools afloat, but one ailing country, whose ship of state is propelled by a corrupt and chauvinistic race headed for doom. Yet similarities in the con man technique are noticeable. Cooley Johnson and Mitchell Pierce would be equally at home on the *Fidèle*, where prey and predator merge into their own fictional reality. The confidence man, as we have seen, demands full confidence of his dupe. When Tam becomes willing prey to Cooley, the cycle begins. Mitchell sets out to con Cooley into taking the black baby off his hands, but Cooley, like Moredock the Indian-Hater, has already worked out his own "Metaphysics of Honky Hating." For his rationale Cooley cites whites' perfidious behavior and their want of conscience for over four hundred years, their theft of black women and double-dealing with black men. He is schooled in the history of his "great-grandaddy" and in the inconsistencies of the present.

Mitchell's overtures are treated by Cooley as seductions to surrender. Take the baby (i.e., be a "good nigger"). Be proud because the baby has a white mother. You must love her—she's white. Only Cooley doesn't love Tam or her child or her world. He loves his brothers, past and present, and has found a unique way to avenge them. Disguised as "Calvin," Cooley leads Mitchell through the labyrinth of distorted black and white relationships, the "funhouse" of American history. Mitchell has difficulty locating the real Cooley because Cooley's friends are wary of the white man's blandishments. Their wariness is bred of experience. What proposition could he have to offer that wouldn't be in their worst interests? For, of course, Mitchell too is a con man, a Yankee peddler of flesh. Usually money is involved in the con game and Mitchell does offer money, although the profit isn't free and clear. "Now, here's fifty dollars for Cooley. And twenty for you," Mitchell says to Calvin. Cooley picks up the money and runs. He's had more experience at the con game than Mitchell, and he's tired of being a loser. His people are tired of losing.

Unlike Melville's Moredock, however, Cooley is not of a murderous mind. His revenge is sexual rather than lethal, characteristically contemporary and satirical. As confidence man he doesn't sell a product, he rejects one—interracial brotherhood. What Cooley does sell is a new state of mind, the new politics of black independence.

The confidence game in *dem* is also a confrontation on the Eldridge Cleaver level of the "Omnipotent Administrator" (white) and the "Supermasculine Menial" (black). The Omnipotent Administrator is "markedly effeminate and delicate by reason of his explicit repudiation and abdication of his body in preference for his mind."[18] On the other hand, "virility, strength and power are associated with the 'Supermasculine Menial.'"[19] In twentieth-century militant fashion, the Supermasculine Menial in *dem* wins out, mainly because he has usurped some brain power functions of the Omnipotent Administrator. Cooley is no longer decapitated (i.e., brainless); he has by his own will performed the necessary surgical procedure, suturing his brain to his body. On the other hand, Mitchell, the bodiless Administrator, has lost not only his sexual potency but also his mental omnipotence. He now finds that the Supermasculine Menial has made inroads into the private island of his mind. The final scene is Kelley's statement of the ultimate end of the Omnipotent Administrator. In it Mitchell takes to the bathtub. Left with the reality of his splintered existence, he submerges himself in the waters (of the womb) in a classical Freudian retreat. He is alone at last, with only his sexual fantasies to fill the darkness. Like *The Confidence Man*, *dem* ends in darkness, but consistent with Kelley's ironic vision, blackness obliterates whiteness.

NOTES

1. Constance Webb, *Richard Wright: A Biography* (New York, 1968), p. 371.
2. Wright took a brief look at the "domestic" black spy in *The Outsider* with the vague shadow of a gunman, Hank, although the character has little substance or credibility: "Menti showed up accompanied by a short, dark Negro who hovered silently behind him, keeping on his hat and overcoat. This man, known as Hank, had a black, blank mask for a face, a grayish scar that went diagonally across his lips and chin, eyes that held a look of chronic hate whose origin seemed to go back to some inaccessible past. Cross knew that the Party had given Menti assistance in the form of this thug to help in spying on him and Eva" (p. 343). Hank and Menti track Cross down together. Which one actually puts the bullet in him is not explicit, but Hank seems the most likely. The "thug" reference is reserved for him and the ominous scar; what's more, he is the only one who is always silent, morose, and trigger happy.
3. Webb, *Richard Wright*, p. 372. Sam Greenlee, in his novel, *The Spook Who Sat by the Door* (1969), depicts a black CIA man, Dan Freeman, as a double agent who, after "integrating" the CIA, uses his cover and his double vision to start the black revolution in America. Freeman's reasoning follows Richard Wright's: "That was why it was an advantage to be black. There were millions of peoples and races in Europe whose centuries of subservience made them culturally perfect as raw material for spying. The nigger was the only natural agent in the United States, the only person whose life might depend, from childhood, on becoming what whites demanded, yet somehow remaining what he was as an individual human being" (p. 109).
4. T. J. Fleming, "Empty Victory," The *New York Times*, October 9, 1967, Sec. 7, p. 66.
5. Webb, *Richard Wright*, p. 378. She also reports one of Wright's experiences with a young man who posed as an agent with an employment bureau, supposedly recruiting French girls to teach the children of rich families back home. "Within a week most black expatriates were joking and whispering about the employment agency man. A few months later there appeared in *Ebony* magazine a photograph in praise of the governess recruiter: he was an agent of the United States Treasury Department and spoke five languages. *Ebony's* revelations of his own suspicions spurred Richard's imagination. He laughed, waved his hands, and described his intention of establishing a Paris Bureau whose job it would be to invent identities for stray black spies" (pp. 378-379).

6. John A. Williams, *The Man Who Cried I Am* (Boston, 1967), p. 13. Further citations will be in the text.

7. Ed Bullins, *The Reluctant Rapist* (New York, 1973), p. 148. In *The System of Dante's Hell*, Baraka places the heretical (which includes black men arrayed against black men) in the deepest circle of hell, even though Dante put them on higher ground (New York, 1963).

8. William Melvin Kelley, *dem* (New York, 1967). Further citations will be in the text.

9. Gustavus Vassa mentions how terrifying it was the first time he was sold to white men. Being enslaved by other blacks meant that he could in most cases understand the language and was among people not too unlike himself. Thrown into company with strange, long-haired creatures of a different color and speaking an unintelligible language was the most frightening experience he had to endure as a child. (Olaudah Equiano, *The Life and Adventures of Olaudah Equiano; or Gustavus Vassa, The African*, From an Account Written by Himself, Abridged by A. Mott [New York, 1829], p. 25.) This verse reflects that fear and explains in part the epithet "devil!" with which Mance later greets Mitchell. Mance is now a teen-age Black Jesuit whose lucubrations are devoted to finding a way to eliminate white people.

10. George Washington is in fact one of the names Cecil Brown gives his protagonist, the newest and brightest con man in black fiction. (See *The Life and Loves of Mr. Jive-ass Nigger*, New York, 1970).

11. Langston Hughes and Arna Bontemps, eds., *The Book of Negro Folklore* (New York, 1958), p. viii.

12. Charles H. Nichols, *Many Thousand Gone: The Ex-Slaves' Account of Their Bondage and Freedom* (Leiden, Netherlands, 1963), p. 36.

13. Robert Bone, "Outsiders," The *New York Times*, Sept. 24, 1967, Sec. 7, p. 36.

14. Leslie Fiedler, *The Return of the Vanishing American* (New York, 1968), p. 82.

15. Two black films, *Shaft* and *Sweet Sweetback's Baadasssss Song*, are evidence that the new mythmakers are addressing themselves to black survival.

16. Richard Wright, *The Outsider* (New York, 1953), p. 129.

17. Newton Arvin, *Herman Melville* (New York, 1950), p. 251.

18. Eldridge Cleaver, *Soul on Ice* (New York, 1968), p. 181.

19. Ibid., p. 180.

9. THE RUNNER AS DEFECTOR

Although the Cold War has left its mark on the term "defector," it is still the most accurate description of the Running Man who dissociates himself voluntarily from military service. Regardless of the time or place, military service for blacks has always been worse than for whites; they have been quartered, paid, equipped, trained, and commanded differently. Harking back to the Civil War, Addison Gayle points out that "only under steady prodding of [Frederick] Douglass, and as a result of Confederate victories, did Lincoln finally accept Negro soldiers—*at less pay, with fewer supplies, under segregated conditions*—in his army" [my emphasis].[1] According to John Hope Franklin, the mortality rate for black soldiers in that war was estimated at more than 38,000, nearly 40 percent greater than for white troops:

The high mortality rate among Negroes is to be explained by several unfavorable conditions. Among them were excessive fatigue details, poor equipment, bad medical care, the recklessness and haste with which Negroes were sent into battle, and the "no quarter" policy with which Confederates fought them.[2]

Yet it appears that blacks, until recently, have not defected from the military—an institution in some ways reminiscent of the "peculiar institution" of slavery—in any sizable number, in spite of their treatment:

Never completely accepted by his white comrades in arms or by his white neighbors at home, the Black soldier has repeatedly gone off to war in defense of a society which has excluded him from its benefits. More often than not, Afro-Americans saw participation in the armed forces as a way of fighting two battles simultaneously—while the real enemy was home-front racism and the real battlefield was in civilian society in the U.S., the Black soldier hoped to win the battle at home through his performance in the Army. Foremost in his mind has been the hope that recognition of his bravery would be rewarded by recognition as a full citizen at home. In every American war, on virtually every American battlefield, Black soldiers have paid a price in flesh and blood for a dream that remained denied.[3]

Contradictory evidence about the incidence of desertion does exist. During the Civil War, General Thomas wrote (December 24, 1863) concerning the 20,830 blacks he had enlisted that "the number of desertions have been few."[4] That was apparently also true in the Revolution and in the War of 1812. The Spanish-American War was qualitatively different. Although many blacks supported the war against Spain, fighting valiantly in Cuba (some as support troops for Roosevelt's "Rough Riders"), they began to balk at fighting the Filipinos, whose struggle for independence was opposed by official American policy and troops. According to Jack Foner, Filipino insurgents made special appeals to black troops to defect from the American army so that they could return home to fight American repression—especially lynching—or to join the insurgents, where they would be treated with equality. Foner reports a difference of opinion between two unnamed historians, one stating that scarcely any troops (only about five blacks) went over to the Filipinos, the other that there was a relatively high rate of desertion among black troops.[5] Robert Mullen indicates that the desertion rate among black troops was indeed high and quotes Stephen Bonsal (whose article in *North American Review*, "The Negro Soldier in War and Peace," 186, June, pp. 325-7, was published in *1907*), to the effect that there was a difference in reasons for desertion from black regiments and from white regiments. While whites generally deserted because of disciplinary opposition, quarrels with officers, or laziness, blacks deserted to join the insurgents. Whatever their number, blacks were apparently welcomed by the Filipino insurgents and some were given major responsibilities. What seems portentous about this experience is the understanding and appeal of the Filipinos who, like Third World peoples today, encouraged the black troops not to be the instruments of their white masters' ambition to oppress another "people of color."[6]

John A. Williams's novel, *Captain Blackman*, published in 1972, sets the background of the history of black involvement in the American military and thus the context for the Running Man as defector from military servitude. As the flight of Ellison's Invisible Man is a creative recapitulation of the black man's history in this country, so is Captain Blackman's symbolic movement in time back through all the wars of American history in which black people have fought and died. Like so many other contributions of black Americans to American life, culture, and history, the participation of blacks in the armed forces of this country has slipped through the pages of history and literature.

Abraham Blackman is the prototype of the black soldier; he is all black men who have played a role in the military history of the United States. As an officer in Vietnam, he suffers a major wound while trying to protect his troops. Like the soldier whom the youth sees propped against a tree in Crane's *The Red Badge of Courage*, he comes "to rest against a stump which forced his face skyward toward the bright blue Viet Nam sky."[7] But Blackman is not dead. As in a dream, he sees the earliest black men, like Peter Salem, Cuff (Whittemore), and Cato (Stedman) fighting with the Colonials, and in a march through history (to Blackman's cadences) he joins them, or men like them, in every battle from the American Revolution to the War of 1812, the Civil War, the Plains Wars, the Spanish-American War, both World Wars (even the war in Spain with the Lincoln Brigade), and the Korean conflict. The present is in Vietnam, and Blackman—a Pomp Blackman was among the black minutemen who participated in the battles of Concord and Lexington—is the character through whose experiences we see the passionate commitment of black men to freedom in each of America's conflicts, experiencing the irony of oppression and discrimination even as they fight and die for the American flag. Blackman is not so much a Runnning Man as he is an instrument of Williams's retelling of American military history. This novel establishes the Running Man as defector from another kind of servitude: it is a change from the slave system, but the expectations for recognition of worth, as well as the restrictions on human freedom, are much the same as those suffered and endured by the slave.

Novels in which the protagonist suffers disaffection from the military cause are not unusual in mainstream white American literature. For a time, Henry, the youth in *The Red Badge of Courage*, becomes a Running Man. Faced with the horrors of actual war, so different from his preconceived heroic vision, he runs like a blind man to escape. Quite by accident, he does not desert permanently. Frederick Henry, in Hemingway's antiwar novel, says his unceremonious farewell to arms and never returns to the scene of battle. Joseph Heller's *Catch-22* ends, somewhat anachronistically with the defection of the protagonist to a Scandinavian country, an event much more common during the Vietnam conflict. Yossarian's flight, whether to escape the horror of war or the horror of the chaotic world of the military, is less important than his recognition that in order to survive, he has to defect. "Yossarian learns that the obligation to keep the spirit alive necessitates removing himself bodily from the system; in order to maintain his spirit, he must remain alive and in rebellion. He must reject Colonel Cathcart's deal, abandon conventional protest, and flee."[8]

Similar situations appear in black writing, but the first to enunciate distinctly the negative attitude of the black soldier toward his experiences is *Home to Harlem* (1928), Claude McKay's first novel. Little is made of Jake Brown's experiences on the battlefield in the First World War because they are nonexistent. In fact, his reason for deserting is that he, as a black man, is not allowed to go to the front to fight as white soldiers do; he is, instead, forced to do the same kind of menial work in the Army that most black men were compelled to do if they wanted to work at all in civilian life. Williams's novel reinforces what McKay wrote, more than forty years earlier, of the Army's plans for blacks in World War I: "For a moment it was clear to Blackman that none of the assignments were worth a damn; that all of them would wind up in the Services of Supply, not in combat" (Williams 1972, 130). When he is about to be shipped to France, one of the white officers tells him: "Ship you out with that Illinois or biggety New York outfit. They're going over first to sweep off the docks in France so white men can fight" (Williams 1972, 133). There were in fact black stevedore battalions, the first of which arrived in France in 1917. While Jake's defection is not the central issue of *Home to Harlem*, it is a significant one. Black critic Hugh Gloster begins his discussion of the novel with a reference to it: "The central character is Jake Brown, who deserts the American Army in Brest because he has to work in labor battalions rather than fight the enemy."[9] On the other hand, Steven Bronz, in his study of three Harlem Renaissance writers, mentions only in passing that Jake is a "returned war veteran."[10]

Jake's frustrating experience in the armed forces of the United States was not isolated; his disenchantment surely was a point of identification for a number of black readers who could easily see his situation not too far from their own. Nevertheless, Jake Brown is not unmanned by his brief sojourn in France; he returns to Harlem to take up his life and his adventures with little if any damage to his ego. Had his introspective and intellectual friend Ray been through such an experience, the novel could conceivably have become a strong indictment against the racism that infected the armed forces, for Ray's function in the novel, according to George Kent, "is to represent a contrast to Jake and to articulate a criticism of Western culture."[11] Clearly racism permeated the military, from petty officers to "Black Jack" Pershing himself—the man whose office issued a memorandum on August 7, 1918, entitled "To the French Military Mission—Secret Information Concerning Black Troops"—a document designed to "sensitize" the French Army to which the black 369th Regiment had been assigned. It stated in part:

1) Prevent the rise of any "pronounced" degree of intimacy between French officers and black officers.
2) Do not eat with Blacks, shake hands, or seek to meet with them outside of military service.
3) Do not commend "too highly" Black troops in the presence of white Americans.[12]

Communiques from Pershing, Commander of the A.E.F., were not all of this sort. Some of his official pronouncements even included commendations of black troops, such as those who served so courageously with the 92nd Division.

After his experiences on the battlefield, the black soldier returned home determined not to take up the old lifestyle. "The American mind," suggested Alain Locke, "must reckon with a fundamentally changed Negro."[13] This "New Negro," as he has been characterized:

began to see the discrepancies between the promise of freedom and his experiences in America. . . . [He] became defiant, bitter, and impatient. It was not the timorous, docile Negro of the past who said, "The next time white folks pick on colored folks, something's going to drop—dead white folks."[14]

A new literary movement developed in this postwar period: political, social, and economic forces seemed to come together to produce the phenomenon known variously as the "Harlem Renaissance," the "Black Renaissance," or the "New Negro Movement."

It is a rare and intriguing moment when a people decide that they are the instruments of history-making and race-building. It is common enough to think of oneself as part of some larger meaning in the sweep of history, a part of some grand design. But to presume to be an actor and creator in the special occurrence of a people's birth (or rebirth) requires a singular self-consciousness. In the opening decades of the twentieth century, down into the first years of the Great Depression, black intellectuals in Harlem had just such a self-concept. These Harlemites were so convinced that they were evoking their people's "Dusk of Dawn" that they believed they marked a renaissance.[15]

The decade, 1919-1929, did indeed seem to signal a cultural and spiritual reawakening among blacks, characterized by a new sense of racial pride, a renewed interest in the past—folk roots as well as African heritage—and a new black attitude, rising in part from the militant nationalism of Garvey's phenomenal Back-to-Africa movement and the World War I experience. Langston Hughes, one of the most prolific, as well as innovative, of the younger writers, declared in "The Negro Artist and the Racial Mountain" (published in *Nation*, June 23, 1926) their cultural independence:

We younger Negro artists who create now intend to express our individual dark-skinned selves without fear or shame. If the white people are pleased, we are glad. If they are not, it doesn't matter. We know we are beautiful. And ugly too. The tom-tom cries and the tom-tom laughs. If colored people are pleased, we are glad. If they are not, their displeasure doesn't matter either. We build our temples for tomorrow, strong as we know them, and we stand on top of the mountain, free within ourselves.

Not all of the artists whose works were culled by Alain Locke and published in *The New Negro: An Interpretation*—Hughes, Jean Toomer, Zora Neale Hurston, Nella Larsen, Rudolph Fisher, Jessie Fauset, Wallace Thurman, Eric Walrond, Countee Cullen, Claude McKay, *et al* are germane to this study. But Claude McKay is, and *Home to Harlem,* to judge by the number of books sold, was the most popular novel of the Harlem Renaissance.

The Depression was a blow to the Harlem Renaissance[16] and the literary opportunities that had given it impetus; it put an end to jobs and to aspirations for economic and social change. The returned veterans experienced few of the benefits they had anticipated even during the halcyon period immediately following the war: they had difficulty in finding employment; they were subject to lynching, riots, varied forms of mob violence (twenty-six different incidents occurred during the "Red Summer of 1919"); even their contributions were deliberately discredited.

The great promise of democratization which should have come from their heroic performance in World War I never materialized, and the literature reflects that disenchantment. Blacks became circumspect about volunteering to serve in a segregated army in the next war. Robert Jones, Chester Himes's protagonist in *If He Hollers Let Him Go* (1945), is more than circumspect; he thinks of military service as the worst possible fate for a black man. Yet he moves inexorably toward that dread destiny. An educated black, leaderman in a Los Angeles shipyard during World War II, Jones is drawn into a perverse relationship with a white southern woman who accuses him of rape. Knowing he has no way of proving his innocence, he tries to escape:

As long as I'd kept moving my mind had remained concentrated on the action. But now a dull hopelessness settled over it, an untempered futility. I felt pressed, cornered, black, as small and weak and helpless as any Negro share-cropper facing a white mob in Georgia. I felt without soul, without mind, at the very end. Everything was useless, flight was useless, nothing I could do would make any difference now.[17]

Like Bigger Thomas, Jones is drawn instinctively back to the heart of the ghetto in which he lives: "They were going to catch me and give me thirty years in prison. For raping a white woman I hadn't even tried to rape" (Himes 1945, 182). They do catch him, but not in the ghetto. They catch him because he's a black man driving in a white neighborhood and he has a gun. For white police it's routine.

Robert Jones is a potential runner, but he is mesmerized by his own feelings of hate for the frustrations he encounters every day of his life trying to live in a racist society, trying to believe, as his light-skinned fiancée does, that he can operate within the limitations set for blacks by white society. When he is confronted by the union steward who tries to settle "Negro problems" in the shipyard in order to "preserve unity on the job" and beat fascism, Jones responds, "What the hell do I care about unity, or the war either, for that matter, as long as I'm kicked around by every white person who comes along? Let the white people get some goddamned unity" (Himes 1945, 108). If Jones steps out of line and responds to racist slurs or tries to protect his Jim Crow gang, he's threatened with the loss of his job deferment: "You're a single boy and they"ll put you in 1A" (Himes 1945, 32). The Army represents the worst possible world: complete entrapment, being at the mercy of the capricious power of the white man. Even in his nightmares the president of the shipyard wears the uniform of an Army general and orders him beaten because he is neither docile nor compliant as "good colored" folks should be.

His worst fears are realized. When his case comes to court, the judge, who is used to filling the armed services with "volunteers," offers him such an opportunity:

"Suppose I give you a break, boy. If I let you join the armed forces—any branch you want—will you give me your word you'll stay away from white women and keep out of trouble?"

I wanted to just break out and laugh . . . and keep on laughing. 'Cause all I ever wanted was just a little thing—just to be a man. But I kept a straight face, got the words through my oversized lips. "Yes sir, I promise."

"Good," he mumbled, standing up. "Don't worry about that charge in Los Angeles." He shook his finger at me, said, "Make a good record, get an honorable discharge. It will do you a lot of good after this war." (Himes 1945, 190)

A number of blacks thought that a "good record" and an honorable discharge would help them finally realize the American dream. Solomon Saunders, Jr., the protagonist in John Oliver Killens's novel, *And Then We Heard the Thunder* (1963), unlike Robert Jones, harbors such illusions when the novel begins; he has gone willingly off to World War II:

It felt good to be part of this. He thought about home and Mama and Mil-
lie . . . and the law school and love and career and future and success. . . .
And the War to Save Democracy. It was his war and he believed in it,
and he would throw all of himself into it. And he would get promoted in a
hurry and assume some leadership.[18]

Solly is repeatedly challenged by Jerry Abraham Lincoln Scott
("Scotty"), the Running Man who wants nothing from the Army but out
and who goes AWOL every chance he can get. Scotty prefers Leavenworth to
the Army and death; he challenges all of Saunders's ambitions, pretensions, and ideas that his participation in the "battle for democracy" will
make a difference either in his life or in the lives of other black people.
Scotty and Bookworm, the prototypes of the "New Negro," are men who
will not prostitute their manhood, men filled with a sense of hopelessness
about America, and they open Saunders's (the"good Negrah's") eyes.[19]
His experiences help: trouble with "cracker" MPs, the Army's Jim Crow
mentality, a beating in a southern jail, segregated facilities, poor training,
drudge labor, heavy and unnecessary losses in battle due to little or no
protection and continued harassment and discrimination in Australia.
There, in Bainbridge, the black men stand and do battle with white troops
deployed against them by the officers of the American military force. A
race war takes place while the "real war" in the Pacific is still in progress.
Solly's metamorphosis is complete; he stands up and with wet eyes stares
down at the bodies:

"I promise you, my buddies, to never forget the way I feel this Monday
morning. I will always hate war with all my heart and all my soul. I
will always fight the men who beat the drums for war in the name of Holy
Patriotism in any nation, any language. I will fight with all the strength
that's in me the goddamn bloated buzzards who profit from this madness." (Killens 1963, 482)

Only a few whites stand with the blacks, one a liberal who, gun in hand,
still mouths the old platitudes: "Maybe we'll really have peace this time.
Maybe after the war is over." But Killens, through Solly, who in spite of
the Army has clearly attained his manhood, envisions things to come:

"If they don't solve *this* question, the whole damn world will be like Bainbridge is this morning! . . .No peace . . . there is no peace till freedom. You
can't make a man slave and have him live in peace with you." (Killens
1963, 483-484)

Written a few years after *And Then We Heard the Thunder*, Killens's
short story "God Bless America" is in some ways a sequel to the novel.[20]

History has moved beyond World War II to the Korean conflict, but the ironies for black soldiers still exist. Joe, like Solly Saunders, has identified himself with American aspirations, and in spite of his wife Cleo's anxieties, is ready to march off to war. The questions that Scotty and Bookworm raised about black men fighting the Japanese in the earlier war are reflected in Cleo's tearful words to Joe: "I don't understand what colored soldiers have to fight for—especially against other colored people" (Killens 1966, 205). Joe, on the other hand, thinks that things have really changed:

"Look, hon, it isn't like it used to be at all. Why can't you take my word for it? They're integrating colored soldiers now. And anyhow, what the hell's the use of getting all heated up about it? I *got* to go. That's all there is to it." (Killens 1966, 206)

A character who resembles Jerry Abraham Lincoln Scott in "God Bless America" is Luke Robinson. He already knows what Joe is about to learn as he gets on the "big white ship" that will take them to Korea. Luke knows that nothing has changed, but Joe is shocked into that realization. The band, which had been playing "God Bless America" as the white troops ascended the gangplank, begins to play "The Darktown Strutters' Ball" as the black troops ascend. Joe is galled and when he looks at the white soldiers on deck waving, smiling, and popping their fingers, he is suddenly ill. Then he hears Luke, cynical but perceptive, say, "I guess Mr. Charley want us to jitterbug onto his pretty white boat. Equal treatment .... We ain't no soldiers, we're a bunch of goddamn clowns" (Killens 1966, 208).

The official government attitude, represented by the military band, and the generally accepted attitude of the white soldiers, represented by the finger-popping white men on the ship, is the same as ever. Luke, in his uneducated yet infinite wisdom, understood this, as did Scotty in *And Then We Heard the Thunder*. Killens's protagonists, in both the novel and the short story, are intelligent, upwardly mobile, aspiring young black men. Solly at first sees himself as one of the few blacks who can move up in Army officialdom with all of the so-called opportunities open to bright young tractable black men. In the next conflict, as it was called, Joe sees himself in somewhat the same situation. When he returns he plans to finish college, to be a lawyer: that is what he's fighting for. The irony of their situation is not immediately apparent to either of them. They are not as worldly wise as the men of the folk, represented in Killens's works by Luke, a street man, and Scotty, a "bad man" ("bad nigger")—with most of the characteristics attributed to that folklore figure, especially fearlessness and courage in the face of physical danger and openness in dealing with whites, regardless of the consequences.

By the end of 1954, *de jure* segregation and discrimination were virtually eliminated from the internal structure of the active military forces, and equal treatment had become official military policy.... Off-post civilian communities, however, remained a constant reminder that the equality of Black soldiers was strictly limited to equality in the defense of American society and did not extend to participation as citizens. Black veterans returning to the United States from Korea were constantly reminded of their inequality in education, employment, and in basic civil and human rights like the right to vote.[21]

Two other novels, *Scarecrow* and *Captain Blackman*, touch on the experience of blacks in the Korean conflict. The section in the latter novel is brief, but it forges another link in the chain of black military experience. The North Koreans, aware of the racial situation in America, devised a special leaflet addressed to black soldiers:

Our battle is not against the exploited, captive Black soldiers of America, but against the white imperialist government that threatens the peace of Asia. Lay down your arms. No harm will come to you. We welcome you as Brothers seeking freedom. (Killens 1966, 282)

Bubba Handy puts a leaflet in his pocket, is listed first as wounded in a costly attack, then as a prisoner of war. Blackman sees a newspaper picture of him years later as one of the leaders of the "Deacons for Defense and Justice." Having successfully defected to the North Koreans, beaten the rap, and been acquitted of collaborating with the Chinese, Bubba proves how "handy" he is at the trickster game. As shrewd as any of the street con men, he dupes the entire United States Army.

In Calvin Hernton's *Scarecrow*, the protagonist is a black writer improbably but aptly named "Scarecrow." He thought that by going into the Army and serving his time he would be assured of an education paid by the GI Bill and save himself from a backbreaking and demeaning factory job with all its harassments.

But the Army turned out to be worse than McFadden's factory. Immediately after training he was sent to Korea where he came under direct supervision of a white man from North Carolina, Sergeant Orville Handson, who had an unmitigable hatred for Negroes. He got so many black soldiers killed by giving suicidal combat orders that the Negroes would have fared better had they been fighting on the other side.[22]

Scarecrow does not defect; he kills Sergeant Handson instead—with a submachine gun. Reflecting years later, after he has killed again and is preparing to take flight from "his" country, he realizes that although he had killed Koreans only to save his life, in his mind he had killed the sergeant many times:

"My country?" he thought. "This ain't never been my country!"

Yet . . . it was his, or it had been his. He had gone and fought for it, killed for it in Korea. And he had hated his countrymen more than the people he had been sent to kill, for it was they, his countrymen and women, both here and over there, who had put a hurting on him at a tender age that would possess and come back to haunt him throughout his living days. There, in Korea, in the blind heat of this hurting he had turned on one of his countrymen . . . his own sergeant, and filled him full of lead. They knew he had done it and not the enemy, as he had reported. They must have known. Why else would they have sent him to "psych" and given him a medical discharge. But now he had killed again. No later than last night he had slaughtered, in the eyes of his country, the most precious thing that a black man can lay hands on.

No. It was not his country any more. (Hernton 1974, 2)

The most precious thing is a white woman, his former wife, who tries to prevent his departure from America: "You aren't going to run away from me with that black bitch and get away with it." He disposes of her in a manner that recalls Bigger Thomas's murder of Mary Dalton: it is far more fastidious—plastic bags for the segmented parts of her body—but no more successful. Scarecrow is a runner who attempts to escape America on a ship, ironically named *Castel Felice,* but he is haunted by the trappings of his past, including the trunk filled with his wife's remains. The voyage is one of violence, attempted exorcism—of the evils of whiteness—and death. Scarecrow never recovers his sanity; he has been infected by the madness endemic to the society and, like Cross Damon, considers himself beyond the bounds of human restraint.

The novel has power and intensity, as black critic Huel Perkins indicates, but several questions linger:

Has America done this to Black people? Has the problem of race so numbed our senses that we are incapable of normal human relationships? Is the whole racial-sexual thing coming apart at the seams? Has it turned Black people into a nation of scarecrows? Maybe these questions best remain unanswered, for if they are answered affirmatively, then civilization is in deep, deep trouble.[23]

The growing climate of disaffection that characterizes fiction dealing with blacks in America's wars reaches its apogee in two works that address themselves to this country's latest dubious commitment in Southeast Asia, *Coming Home* and *Runner Mack*. Both novels have running men as defectors.

Coming Home, by George Davis, published in 1971, is one of the few Afro-American novels that deals specifically with the war in Indochina. Although its title is reminiscent of Claude McKay's *Home to Harlem*, and although one of the three main characters, Childress, does come home, the novel has none of the joy of return that characterized the earlier work. Although Jake Brown is disenchanted by his experience, or lack of experience, in the war in France, he does return to Harlem to take up his life in a much less complex and frightening world than that depicted by Davis. Just as there are two black characters in *Home to Harlem*, the educated black and the natural man (cf. the Harvard Black and the Harlem Black in William Kelley's *Dunfords Travels Everywheres*), there are two contrasting black characters in *Coming Home*. Ben is a Harvard-trained black man; Childress, a Texan who quit college to join the Air Force. Childress is the only one of the three fighter pilots whose lives we follow in Davis's novel who actually does return to the United States. The irony of the title then becomes clear: Childress comes home to the same conditions that existed when he left, and after he kills a white policeman, his "home" is prison. Stacy, the third character, who rooms with the two black men in Thailand, is white. He dies in Vietnam, a victim of his own sexual fantasies and a true believer in the "American way." In spite of his friendship with Childress, Stacy falls victim to the unspoken racist attitudes and beliefs about the fascination black men have for white women. When Stacy hears that Roxanne, his girlfriend, has visited Childress in prison, he is convinced that she will be unfaithful to him. Although he has been looking forward to his final flying mission, he becomes so depressed that it is clear he no longer cares to go home. During the last mission he fantasizes their betrayal:

I see a line of trucks, camouflaged against a row of huts. I steady the pip and squeeze the trigger as I streak downward. It's the goddam Jews and women who are betraying the white race. I think about Childress and Roxanne in bed together. My firing jolts me and I seem to hang for a moment, while the backward thrust of the gun battles the forward push of the engines.[24]

Stacy's liberalism gives way when his manhood is threatened. He confuses sexuality and civilization, morality and murder:

I think civilization itself is in danger right here in the mud of Vietnam and you've got to fight even if no one else wants to help. The world is full of Gooks and niggers and they'll tear down everything the white man has ever built, I say to myself, almost as if I'm talking to Roxanne, not to get her to agree with me, but just so she has it for the record. I wouldn't touch her now with a ten-foot pole. I don't want to come within miles of her. She's never even going to know where I am. I hope there's a lying letter from her waiting for me when I get back, so I can tear it up. (Davis 1971, 201)

Stacy, however, does not get back. Presumably he chooses to make this his last mission on earth, and he dies amid the wreckage of his plane, "twirling earthward and hitting the wet floor of the valley, which we have already saturated with fire" (Davis 1971, 204). Stacy's death is as meaningless as the death of the faceless Vietnamese on whom he and the other fighter pilots have rained anonymous bombs.

Coming Home is a spare, tightly written novel without embellishments. Each chapter is told from the point of view of the speaker with no authorial interference: "Thus each character speaks from his or her own psychic prison within the greater dome of complicity."[25] Davis's view of the Vietnam war and the corruption and death it has spawned is convincing and powerful. Black men have been corrupted by it as well. They have taken up the pejorative terms used by the whites. Childress, going on his last mission as the novel opens, tells Stacy: "Yeah, got to go kill my last Gook" (Davis 1971, 4). He wants Ben and Stacy to see his last performance, and seems totally unaware that "Gook" has the same degrading connotation as "Nigger" (in Williams's novel, the captain tries to educate his men away from such dehumanizing terms). Childress is unaware of his own motives for sabotaging Ben's chances of "inheriting" Damg, his Thai prostitute, when he returns to the States: "You said you wasn't going to let a Harvard-trained dude inherit the best whore in Thailand" (Davis 1971, 30). When Stacy asks how Childress will prevent Ben from "inheriting" Damg, he says that he has hidden communist papers in her room. "When they find the literature, they'll swear she's a communist. See? And no red-blooded Amurrican, including Ben, will be allowed within a mile of her" (Davis 1971, 30). Childress does not realize that he will eventually suffer for his actions—the papers he hides in Damg's room will be used against him in the murder case the police in Baltimore later put together. Implicit in the "inheritance" process is the collusion of the men in Vietnam in the dehumanizing of a people. Davis never comments in his own voice; the indictment is subtle but clear.

Ben is the only Running Man of this uneasy trio. He refuses either to stay in Vietnam or to return home, although he has flown countless missions and has acquiesced for so long in the meaningless deaths of so many "colored" people. Ben even has a wife back home to whom he feels relatively little loyalty, and like Yossarian in *Catch-22* when he leaves for Sweden,[26] after he takes flight from the Vietnam debacle, we never see him again.

Ben is slow to reach the level of consciousness achieved by some black men who either entered the Army already politicized or developed very quickly into a force for change after their induction: Joe Miles and Andrew Pulley, for example, who were among the Fort Jackson 8— GIs who spoke out against the war.[27] He seems unaware of the pronouncements of such divergent leaders as Malcolm X and Martin Luther King regarding the immorality of the war itself and, as Malcolm insisted, the hypocrisy and criminality of a government that was

supposed to be a democracy, supposed to be for freedom . . . when they want to draft you and put you in the Army and send you to Saigon to fight for them—and then you've got to turn around and all night long discuss how you're going to just get a right to register and vote without being murdered.[28]

Too late, Ben realizes how much he has grown to despise America for everything it has taught him:

I shiver for a moment, knowing that I don't want to go back to America with all this hatred in me.

I should never have come into the war but I came like a sheep. During all my life in America I've been led to loving the wrong things and hating the wrong things, like I was nothing more than a goddam sheep. (Davis 1971, 18)

His awareness comes through the unreality of the experience of killing without seeing the killed:

For me this war is like Harvard. Nothing in it seems real. Everything is abstract. Everything is an argument or a question . . . . When it's possible to kill without seeing blood, then it's possible to kill without remorse or guilt. (Davis 1971, 17)

In spite of Childress's attempts to keep Damg and Ben apart, they finally get together and go to Bangkok. From there, Ben defects. His early moments of wondering what would happen if he "disappeared forever into the human and bamboo jungles of Asia" (Davis 1971, 27), develop into decision when he meets a black infantryman who has been AWOL for twenty-one days. He tells Ben that he made his decision to desert after he killed a Vietnamese boy who wanted to give him a shoeshine. Suspecting

THE RUNNER AS DEFECTOR / 141

that the boy had a bomb in the shoeshine box, he shot the child in the back when he ran. But all he found in the box was shoe polish: "Not a goddam thing but shoe polish. I went back to the base and packed my shit and left. I ain't ever gon' kill no more innocent people, man. And I ain't going to no jail either" (Davis 1971, 169). Ben wishes the soldier good luck and sits down to think "about all the black men who have been hitting the road, catching trains. Then I think about all the black men in prisons or on Southern prison farms. I try and weigh one group against another" (Davis 1971, 170). Then he packs his things and leaves.

Peter Rand characterizes *Coming Home* as "our" war novel:

It suggests much more in its brief episodes than the curious lassitude of aerial killing and the little drama of the three protagonists. It suggests that oppression possesses a limitless hierarchy, that the Vietnam war contains metaphorically, the image of our own social death. It suggests that we are alone with our misconceptions. So of course it does not celebrate courage, or physical endurance, or nobility among men, or even, evil among men. *Coming Home* is a sure, swift design for the death of feeling.[29]

The protagonist of *Runner Mack*, by Barry Beckham, published in 1972, is a naïve young black man from the South, Henry Adams. The Running Man defector does not appear in this novel until the second half. He is Runnington Mack (known also as Runner and the Run), whom Henry meets after he has been drafted into the Army to serve in Vietnam and who becomes a kind of mentor to him at the most important stage of his growth to maturity. Each experience in the novel is a kind of education: the book seems, on one level, to be a parody of *The Education of Henry Adams*, one of the most famous of "first family" autobiographies; *Runner Mack* is the reeducation of Henry Adams—black—a member no doubt of one of slavery's first families. Henry's father has slavishly accommodated himself to white society—"All his life holding back and shucking and jiving, trying, making me think and act just like him"[30]—a "good Negro."

The novel is divided according to the learning stages of Henry's life after he has reached the North, the land of opportunity, aspiring to "make it" in the major leagues:

This is how it would be, he thought, and his wrists were hot, his underwear felt sticky, for he wasn't sure it was true, what they were saying about opportunities and straight to the top. He was going down the plank and he didn't know what to expect. How would Momma Lou advise him? This was worse than trying to steal home, it was a larger dilemma than being run down between second and first, and far worse than guarding the bag when a cleat-spitting runner was heading toward you. Scared as scared could be. Pilot, oh pilot me. (Beckham 1972, 25)

With his heritage of accommodation, Henry is used to being pushed around, ignored, made to feel unimportant. He cannot force the custodian of the tenement in which he and his wife Beatrice live to stop ignoring his complaints of no heat and leaking ceilings; he waits interminably for word on his baseball contract; and he is muscled in the streets and made to feel the coon (someone shouts "Stepin Fetchit" at him) as he tries desperately to get to a job interview at Home Manufacturing Company. Yet Henry is one of the least aware of heroes. Like the Invisible Man, he knows that there are things about the world he should know, and he persists in trying to understand, to probe, as he does at Home, a place not totally unlike Liberty Paints. The difference is that the powers behind the latter know that what they are producing is important to the status quo. Liberty's "pure" white paint succeeds in making the contributions of blacks (the ten black drops) invisible: it is the national whitewash. What is more, the profits from the industrial complex are made by exploitation of all workers, but especially blacks, who are consigned to the subbasement where the most onerous labor is performed, and duped (like Brockway) into not only accepting that role but also zealously protecting it.

The powers behind Home have taken a step toward "token" hiring, a reflection of latter-day "equal opportunity" practices enforced by law during the sixties—the acquisition of showcase blacks. Beckham's satirical but subtle method recalls the acquisition of black people at an earlier stage of our economic history. Peters of Personnel (Henry mistakenly says, "Glad to meet you, Peter, " and then is frightened that his *faux pas* will cost him the job) brings in three "globes of smoke" to interview Henry: A. L. Klein, B. J. Kind, and M. O. Baby.

"Let's see your teeth, Henry . . . open up."
"He's got strength" [feeling his biceps].
"Do you believe in . . . do you believe in God, my boy?"
"Of course, A. L., don't be stupid. They all believe in God. Of course he does. Uh, have you been sick lately, Henry? I mean, are you healthy and fit? Have you had the smallpox?"
"What can you do best, Henry—work with your hands, huh?"
"Have you ever stolen, Henry? You wouldn't take any of our machinery out of here, would you?"
"Oh, he looks honest, men, but Henry, answer me this—would you run away if you didn't like the work?" (Beckham 1972, 21-22)

As Jim Walker suggests, Klein, Kind, and Baby are

the slave owners at a slave auction [Henry is reminded of an "auctioneer's verbal magic" as he listens to them] examining and testing a piece of merchandise they will "buy," in this case Henry (for Home Manufacturing). And they literally do "buy" Henry into one of the most impersonal, cold, and dehumanizing factories you are ever likely to see in fiction.[31]

Walker sees an analogy between the imagery of the factory section in *Runner Mack* and that in Orwell's *1984* and Forster's "The Machine Stops." Certainly the theme of dehumanization is pervasive in contemporary literature, with the factory as metaphor for the deadening of modern man's spirit through mechanistic twentieth-century society. Beckham adds another dimension. Not only does he show how senseless, stupid, and demeaning the factory system is to the well-being of the total society, he clearly demonstrates that blacks are still *only* slaves who are bought, sold, and threatened with "Don't try to run away, you can't escape!" (Beckham 1972, 23)

Henry does try to leave Home, particularly after his encounter with Mr. Boye (Beckham's most incisive and symbolic oxymoron) who confesses to Henry that he has no idea *what* they are doing, what they are making; he only knows that he has been supervising for forty years and been paid for it. The information is dangerous; Henry overhears Boye and Peters discussing their suspicions of him:

". . . The other workers start thinking, it'll be a mess. We'll have a shitstorm on our hands. If it hits the fan—"

"I told you not to hire that bastard. He looked suspicious to me during the interview. I didn't like his teeth." (Beckham 1972, 107)

Thinking is the greatest threat to the system, a process that, once begun, can undermine the entire basis of society. Henry knows he has to extricate himself, but he does not know how, nor does he have a guide. Neither his father nor Beatrice can play that role. The Army intervenes and he moves from one mad, dehumanizing way of life to another.

In the middle of a warm conjugal night—the night he and Beatrice are going to communicate with each other, finally—he receives a note:

You have been drafted to help fight the war. We are waiting for you outside. Report immediately—right now. (Beckham 1972, 128)

Beatrice tries to keep Henry from leaving, but he dashes wildly out of bed: "I have to fight for my country—it's our country. We live in it. How do you expect me to play ball for a team if they know I didn't want to help keep this country safe? I'm a man" (Beckham 1972, 129). Beatrice runs nakedly after him but Henry is whisked off to war in a transport truck marked MILITARY, waiting for him outside his door. It's another serio-comic scene, skillfully understated, like the one of Henry running madly down the street, being hit by a truck, crawling into Home Manufacturing and having the whole thing passed off as though it were a usual occurrence (Peters: "Oh, I'm so sorry, Henry. The streets are damned crowded though, aren't they? Did you have any trouble finding the place?")

We know how serious the intent is when Henry is catapulted into the "Alaskan War," and the second section of the novel.

I love you and Momma for all that you've done for me, but I can't go on like this. I want some control over my life.... I don't know precisely where I'll go with it, but I want it .... It's not your fault that I'm like this and that I have to write from the battlefield of Alaska while in some tank, and we're about to gun down some beautiful animals. But you, Daddy would probably go along with it. (Beckham 1972, 131)

When Runner Mack appears, he becomes the guide for whom Henry has been searching without realizing it. The "Run" is sure, positive, unhesitant. He is like Scotty and Luke, streetwise, black and "bad." He says aloud what Henry has been thinking:

"Why should I kill somebody that I don't dislike? I don't have anything against these people. Who are they? What did they do to me?" (Beckham 1972, 149)

The same question is asked by other potential defectors, but Mack is different—he has a plan. First he politicizes Henry, exposing the hypocrisy of Christianity, the decadence of white morality, the brutality of white aggression:

We been believing in their God and the golden rule all our lives while Chuck has been laughing at us and acting like a beast. What's it done for us, Henry? Huh? Can you answer me that with your black self? Can you tell me why we still listen to that jive dogma while whitey acts the mad hypocrite? We can't follow them anymore, Henry. . .They've fucked up everything, they've killed and mangled and transgressed all their lives, and we can't become a part of it. We must remain humane and spiritual within this madness." (Beckham 1972, 154).

Henry is convinced; he breaks with the old notions of his father, the "Negro" past, and joins Mack in a revolutionary plot to bomb the White House: "He would be a new man, a new black man; awakened, sore, angry, strong" (Beckham 1972, 196). It is a part of Mack's larger plan. First they appropriate a "chopper," make good their escape from "Alaska" and go to join the revolutionary force that Mack has set up across the country. That force somehow disintegrates and the plan fails dismally. Mack, the source of Henry's newfound strength, blackness, and manhood disintegrates also:

"There are no answers, Henry, that's the whole problem. I just figured it out. There are no answers. We just keep trying and planning and it doesn't mean anything. History keeps going and we keep trying and nothing happens and somebody else says, 'I'll do it,' and they try and nothing really changes. There are no answers, Henry. We just keep going on and on, hoping it will make sense, but it never does, does it?" (Beckham 1972, 211)

With Runner Mack's death and the end of the revolutionary plan, Henry becomes a runner:

He didn't know where he was going, but he knew he had to run, because it was rapidly making little sense and he knew that if he was still for a minute to digest everything he would have to give up. He knew if he had stayed in that bathroom and begun to contemplate what Runner Mack's hanging himself had meant to him, Runner, then he, Henry, would be drained. And he couldn't be drained. He had to run, search, look, fight— but more than anything, not give up. (Beckham 1972, 212)

Neither desertion from the Army nor Mack's plan to eliminate exploitation and oppression—by white society, civilian and military—sustains Henry. His metamorphosis from "good Negro" to revolutionary through his contact with Runner Mack apparently has limited success. Struck earlier by a truck on the way to the slave system of the factory, he is struck and apparently killed by another after the plan fails and Mack dies. Perhaps Beckham is saying that black men need something more than plans that are doomed to failure. They need to discover some tangible means to cope with the environment of violence and racism and then their education will be complete. Henry does not make that discovery; in his blind flight he does not even hear the voices admonishing him to look out:

He glanced to his right and saw the truck bearing down on him, the shiny rectangles of a grille, the two figures in the cab, the pumpkin-sized glass headlamps, the engine groaning, and the mouth of a fender smiling at him, smiling at him . . . smiling. (Beckham 1972, 213)

Walker considers the first half of the novel superior to the second "in its artistry, in its introduction of themes, in its use of language and its presentation of characterization."[32] Certainly the conception of Home Manufacturing and the characterizations of Boye, the president, an ugly shell of a man who can neither walk alone nor make himself understood without interpreters but who controls the company, and the hear-no-evil, see-no-evil monkeys, Klein, Kind, and Baby, are as caustic, imaginative, and telling as those in any contemporary satire. The factory sequences are in some ways as cinematic as *Modern Times*, with Henry the Chaplinesque version of the desk-bound automaton. But the "Alaskan War" is the ultimate absurdity and Beckham's symbols evoke a landscape of lunacy. Black men are again sent into battle ill-trained; this time they are expected to kill some of nature's most beautiful creatures so that an unseen enemy will starve:

"Gentlemen, good morning, gentlemen, and welcome to Birthday Pass, Alaska, and welcome to Alaska, too. Gentlemen, I am your CO, call me captain, Captain Nevins [Alan?]. Gentlemen, we don't have time to train you. We're here to fight . . . Our mission is to destroy these ginks, these sloop-eyes, or the next thing you know they'll be in our fuckeen backyards." (Beckham 1972, 133)

The derogatory language used by the absurd captain (a John Wayne type) makes the locale of the war clear. They are of course surrounded by whiteness—the whiteness of the landscape, the snow bluffs— it is a white man's war. Henry "had never see so much white before in his life—not even on the largest cotton field." Their only answer is to change the terrain and to make a black man's war.

Williams's Captain Blackman envisions a different end: black men have changed; they lean on history and see a new light. They successfully defeat United States military power by safely neutralizing the American nuclear missile force from the African continent. The American commander, disbelieving, says: "We're defenseless. You've been in a war for hundreds of years and you've just lost it. Don't tell me about the Soviets. You don't understand. You've just lost the war to niggers" (Williams 1972, 310). Blackman—black men of Africa and America—have come together to change the world; they have, as Melvin Van Peebles's Sweetback threatened, come back to "collect some dues."

John Killens had suggested a similar possibility at the end of *And Then We Heard the Thunder*, when Solly Saunders thinks: "Perhaps the New World *would* come raging out of Africa and Asia, with a new and different dialogue that was people-oriented. What other hope was there?" (Killens 1963, 485). The world wakes up to sunshine and hope: it is Don L. Lee's "walk the way of the new world"—not a threat but a promise.

NOTES

1. Addison Gayle, Jr., *The Black Situation* (New York, 1970), p. 93. Two of Douglass's sons were part of the Fifty-fourth Massachusetts Regiment that refused for one year to draw its pay in order to protest the fact that black privates earned only $7 per month and $3 for clothing, while white privates earned $13 per month and received $3.50 for clothing.
2. John Hope Franklin, *From Slavery to Freedom*, 2nd ed. (New York, 1956), p. 290.
3. Robert W. Mullen, *Blacks in American Wars: The Shift in Attitudes from the Revolutionary War to Vietnam* (New York, 1973), p. 9.
4. Quoted in Leslie H. Fishel, Jr., and Benjamin Quarles, *The Negro American, A Documentary History* (New York, 1967), p. 232.
5. Jack D. Foner, *Blacks and the Military in American History: A New Perspective* (New York, 1974), p. 92.
6. Mullen, *Blacks in American Wars*, p. 40. The Germans tried to encourage black troops to desert during World War I but apparently were unsuccessful.
7. John A. Williams, *Captain Blackman* (New York, 1972), p. 5. Further citations will be in the text.
8. Thomas Blues, "The Moral Structure of *Catch-22*" in *Joseph Heller's Catch-22: A Critical Edition*, ed. Robert M. Scotto (New York, 1973), p. 557.
9. Hugh M. Gloster, *Negro Voices in American Fiction* (New York, 1948), p. 163. The only other black World War I defector I have been able to identify appeared in a British-made film, *Jericho* (released in this country under the title *Dark Sands*) in 1937. Paul Robeson starred in the role of a black corporal who deserts the AEF while stationed in France because he is court-martialed and given an excessive sentence for accidentally killing another non-commissioned officer while trying to rescue his men. The film was certainly rare for the period. Jericho not only effectuates his escape, but he also acquires a white Gunga Din (Wallace Ford) with whom he sails to Africa, a beautiful African wife and, because of his skills and intelligence, becomes a respected leader.
10. Steven Bronz, *Roots of Negro Racial Consciousness, The 1920s: Three Harlem Renaissance Authors* (New York, 1964), p. 80.
11. George Kent, *Blackness and the Adventure of Western Culture* (Chicago, 1972), p. 47.
12. Mullen, *Blacks in American Wars*, p. 44. Nathan Huggins indicates that this memorandum also warned against black and white fraternization "lest Negroes rape French women." (*Harlem Renaissance* [New York, 1971], p. 54.)
13. Alain Locke, "The New Negro," in *The New Negro: An Interpretation* (New York, 1970), p. 8. (Originally published 1925.)
14. Franklin, *From Slavery to Freedom*, p. 490.
15. Huggins, *Harlem Renaissance*, p. 3.
16. "Although the loss of white patronage resulting from the stock market crash critically wounded the movement, it produced writers who were to persist and whose consciousnesses were to become an essential metaphor for black realities of subsequent periods as they remained open to new tensions." Kent, *Blackness and the Adventure*, p. 35.
17. Chester Himes, *If He Hollers Let Him Go* (New York, 1945), p. 182. Further citations will be in the text. The title comes from the old children's rhyme:

>   Eeeny meeny miney moe
>   Catch a nigger by the toe
>   If he hollers let him go
>   Eeny meeny miney moe.

A variant on this chant is a Texas version:

Eeny meeny miney moe
Catch a nigger by the toe
If he hollers, make him pay
Fifty dollars every day.

Other regional variations may reflect the same virulent racism.

18. John Oliver Killens, *And Then We Heard the Thunder* (New York, 1963), p. 24. Further citations will be in the text.
19. Book review, *Freedomways* III, no. 2 (February 1963): 23.
20. John Oliver Killens, "God Bless America" in *American Negro Short Stories*, ed. John Henrik Clarke (New York, 1966). Further citations will be in the text. This story is almost word-for-word the ending section of Part II, *And Then We Heard The Thunder*. The war has changed, and the names, but the situation is the same: the white ship, "God Bless America," "The Darktown Strutters' Ball," and racism. (See pp. 247-250.)
21. Mullen, *Blacks in American Wars*, p. 61.
22. Calvin Hernton, *Scarecrow* (New York, 1974), p. 45. Further citations will be in the text.
23. Huel D. Perkins, Review, *Black World* (June 1975): 93.
24. George Davis, *Coming Home* (New York, 1971), p. 200. Further citations will be in the text.
25. Peter Rand, Book Review, *New York Times* (January 9, 1972), p. 7.
26. Maya Angelou's screenplay for *Georgia Georgia*, which was shot on location in Stockholm, concerns itself with the plight of blacks in Sweden who have either deserted from or refused induction into the armed services.
27. See Fred Halstead, *GIs Speak Out Against the War: The Case of the Ft. Jackson 8* (New York, 1970). Interviews with participants.
28. Malcolm X, "The Black Revolution," in *Malcolm X Speaks*, ed. George Breitman (New York, 1965), p. 144.
29. Rand, Book Review, p. 7.
30. Barry Beckham, *Runner Mack* (New York, 1972), p. 164. Further citations will be in the text.
31. Jim Walker, Book Reviews, *Black Creation* 4, no. 2 (Winter 1973): 62.
32. Walker, Book Reviews, p. 62.

BIBLIOGRAPHICAL ESSAY

Slave Narratives and Related Works

One of the best collections of slave narratives is in the Boston Public Library.[1] William Lloyd Garrison's copy of *Running a Thousand Miles to Freedom; or the Escape of William and Ellen Craft from Slavery* (1860), with an inscription by the Crafts, is in that collection. The Schomburg Collection of the New York Public Library and the Spingarn Collection at Howard University are excellent sources for research, as are the libraries at Hampton Institute, Harvard, Brown, Fisk, and Cornell Universities, and Oberlin College. A new and healthy interest in this unique genre has produced anthologies[2] such as those edited by Arna Bontemps, *Great Slave Narratives* (Boston, 1969), Gilbert Osofsky, *Puttin' on Ole Massa: The Slave Narratives of Henry Bibb, William Wells Brown, and Solomon Northup* (New York, 1969), and Julius Lester, *To Be a Slave* (New York, 1971) in convenient paperback editions. The Bontemps book includes: *The Interesting Narrative of the Life of Olaudah Equiano, or Gustavus Vassa, the African, Written by Himself* (1789), *The Fugitive Blacksmith, or Events in the History of James W. C. Pennington, Pastor of a Presbyterian Church, New York, Formerly a Slave in the State of Maryland, United States* (1849), and *Running a Thousand Miles to Freedom*.

Very few anthologies of Afro-American writing now appear without selections from one or two slave narratives. The most popular by far is the extraordinary *Narrative of the Life of Frederick Douglass, an American Slave, Written by Himself* (1845) which was published in an updated version in 1855 as *My Bondage and My Freedom*, subdivided into Part 1,

"Life as a Slave," and Part 2, "Life as a Freeman." A third expanded and revised version was published in 1882 as *The Life and Times of Frederick Douglass, Written by Himself*. (The original version is now available in an extremely useful small paperback edition.) Chapter 10 from the original *Narrative* (1845) appears in Houston A. Baker, Jr.'s *Black Literature in America* (1971). *Black American Literature, 1760-Present* (1971), edited by Ruth Miller, has selections from Douglass's *Narrative*, as well as from those of Austin Seward (1857), Solomon Bayley (1825), Henry "Box" Brown (1851), Henry Bibb (1849), and Moses Roper (1840). *Cavalcade; Negro American Writings from 1760 to the Present* (Boston, 1971), edited by Arthur P. Davis and Saunders Redding, has selections from Gustavus Vassa's *Narrative* and one from Douglass's *Life and Times* (1882 version). Davis and Redding also include an excerpt from Elizabeth Keckley's *Behind the Scenes; or Thirty Years a Slave and Four Years in the White House* (1868; see my Introduction page 9). *Afro-American Writing: An Anthology of Prose and Poetry* (New York, 1972), edited by Richard Long and Eugenia Collier and published in two volumes, includes Chapter 1 of Samuel Ringgold Ward's *Autobiography of a Fugitive Negro*. Ward himself was three years old when his parents escaped from slavery, but as he points out, according to slave law, the child follows the condition of his mother, and his mother was not free when she gave birth to him. In this country, therefore, he was always subject to the threat of recapture and reenslavement. *Black Writers of America: A Comprehensive Anthology* (New York, 1972), edited by Richard Barksdale and Keneth Kinnamon, contains a selection from Gustavus Vassa's *Narrative* and Chapter 10 from the original version of Douglass's *Narrative*.

"Plantation Slavery in the Antebellum South" in Part 3 of *Blacks in America: Bibliographical Essays* by James M. McPherson, et al. (Garden City, N.Y., 1971) gives additional information about other collections of narratives: e.g., *Lay My Burden Down: A Folk History of Slavery* (Chicago, 1945), edited by B. A. Botkin from the Federal Writers Project interviews of ex-slaves during the New Deal period. Norman Yetman, editor of *Life Under the "Peculiar Institution": Selections from the Slave Narrative Collection* (New York, 1970), and Julius Lester, *To Be A Slave*, also made use of these interviews compiled during the years 1936-1938. *The Unwritten History of Slavery: Autobiographical Accounts of Negro Ex-Slaves* (Nashville, 1945, reprinted Washington, 1968) in two volumes by Fisk University, was compiled by scholars who interviewed ex-slaves in the twenties and thirties. And *The American Slave: Composite Autobiography* (Westport, Conn., 1971–), George P. Rawick's nineteen-volume collection and study in two series, contains a critical introduction and narratives from seventeen different states.

Charles H. Nichols's *Many Thousand Gone: The Ex-Slaves' Account of Their Bondage and Freedom*, a very useful study of the slave narrative, was published in Leiden, Netherlands in 1963 and was not, until a few years ago, well known in this country. Professor Nichols's experiences as a black American scholar and his decision to live for some time as an expatriate in Germany (see his account in *The Black Expatriates*, edited by Ernest Dunbar and published in 1968) explain, in part, the frustrations of a black scholar in America. Fortunately, *Many Thousand Gone* has been available in paperback (Bloomington, Indiana, 1969) for several years. The opening chapter of Sidonie Smith's *Where I'm Bound: Patterns of Slavery and Freedom in Black American Autobiography* (1974), a critical study of black autobiographies, is entitled "Flight." That chapter is an examination of the composition of the slave narrative as a way to freedom for the exslave through literary expression. The important relationship between the slave narrative and the autobiographical impulse in black writing is receiving more recognition and attention. Saundra Towns's "Black Autobiography and the Dilemma of Western Artistic Tradition," *Black Books Bulletin*, Vol. 2, No. 1 (Spring 1974), divides major narratives and autobiographies into two categories: the engaged (Douglass, DuBois, Malcolm X) and the disengaged (Wright, Baldwin, Himes) and places Gwendolyn Brooks's autobiography, *Report from Part 1*, into the context of black historical and literary tradition. The following is a list of representative black autobiographies of this century, beginning with Booker T. Washington's *Up From Slavery*, which has been characterized by some critics as the "last of the slave narratives."

Up From Slavery, Booker T. Washington (1901)
The Souls of Black Folk, W. E. B. DuBois (1903) (Personal Essays)
Born to Be, Taylor Gordon (1929)
Along This Way, James Weldon Johnson (1933)
A Long Way From Home, Claude McKay (1937)
The Big Sea, Langston Hughes (1940)
Dusk of Dawn: An Essay Toward an Autobiography of a Race Concept,
     W. E. B. DuBois (1940)
Dust Tracks on a Road, Zora Neale Hurston (1941)
No Day of Triumph, J. Saunders Redding (1942)
Black Boy, Richard Wright (1945)
A Man Called White, Walter White (1948)
Notes of a Native Son, James Baldwin (1955)
I Wonder as I Wander: An Autobiographical Journey, Langston Hughes
     (1956)
Here I Stand, Paul Robeson (1958)

Nobody Knows My Name, James Baldwin (1961)
The Fire Next Time, James Baldwin (1963) (Autobiographical Essays)
Long Old Road, Horace R. Cayton (1963)
Manchild in the Promised Land, Claude Brown (1965)
The Autobiography of Malcolm X, Malcolm X and Alex Haley (1965)
Home: Social Essays, Imamu Baraka (LeRoi Jones) (1966)
Black and Conservative: The Autobiography of George S. Schuyler,
   George S. Schuyler (1966)
Soul on Ice, Eldridge Cleaver (1968)
Autobiography: A Soliloquy, W. E. B. DuBois (1968)
Coming of Age in Mississippi, Anne Moody (1969)
I Know Why the Caged Bird Sings, Maya Angelou (1970)
Soledad Brother: The Prison Letters of George Jackson, George Jackson
   (1970)
Beneath the Underdog, Charles Mingus (1971) (Semi-autobiographical)
*Gemini: An Extended Autobiographical Statement on My First Twenty-
   Five Years of Being a Black Poet,* Nikki Giovanni (1971)
The Quality of Hurt: The Autobiography of Chester Himes, Chester
   Himes, Vol. 1 (1972)
Report from Part One, Gwendolyn Brooks (1972)
Angela Davis: An Autobiography, Angela Davis (1974)
Gather Together in My Name, Maya Angelou (1974)

Most autobiographies listed are by persons engaged in literature or the
other arts. Although it is possible to see these works in the context of traditional American autobiographies, one difference is clearly apparent: the
success theme in most instances is replaced by the theme of survival.

Criticism by Black Scholar Critics

Just as the Afro-American writer has been absent from traditional
American literature courses, so has the Afro-American critic been excluded from literary scholarship. "Even when their subject has been literature
by Afro-American writers, black critics have failed to make America see
them, to say nothing of reading or hearing their words" (Darwin T. Turner,
"Afro-American Literary Critics: An Introduction" in *The Black Aesthetic*
[New York, 1972], edited by Addison Gayle). Some bibliographies are
available, but most do not identify the black critic, divulge his background
or indicate the number of years he has been engaged in serious scholarly
work. There is a one-volume reference by Ann Allen Shockley, *Living
Black Authors* (New York, 1973), which includes black authors as a total

group and does, in part, fill this need. Turner's own bibliography, *Afro-American Writers* (New York, 1970) focuses on the literature and literary scholarship of Afro-Americans but also includes both black and white critics.

"Afro-American Literary Critics: An Introduction," cited above, provides a brief history of Afro-American critics, discusses the field of criticism, and gives some important insight into the nature of the problem. In that essay, Turner points out that the mass of literate Americans do not read the publications of black critics and therefore do not know them, that few anthologies include black criticism, and that black critics have been denied opportunity, or at least have not been encouraged, to present their works in the most respected media. (It is also true that they do not know the major black journals, periodicals, and newspapers where critical reviews and scholarly works are likely to be published.)

As Turner suggests, black American critics can offer insights into the language, styles, and meanings intended by black writers because, for one thing, they have had the experience of living as black people in the United States. However, such insights can only be shared if the reader has access to them. This section is designed to familiarize the reader with names of some black scholar/critics, as well as their major critical works in book form, and black periodicals in which their work has appeared.

While not mutually exclusive, there are three major categories of critics: the academic and historical critics, Black Aesthetic critics, and critics who are primarily creative writers.[3] Among the academic and historical critics are: Benjamin Brawley, Sterling Brown, Alain Locke, Saunders Redding, Nick Aaron Ford, Hugh Gloster, Blyden Jackson, John Hope Franklin, Margaret Just Butcher, Ernest Kaiser, James Emanuel, W. Edward Farrison, Darwin T. Turner, Nathan Huggins, Richard Long, Helen Johnson, Eugenia Collier, Richard Barksdale, George Kent, Stephen Henderson, Houston A. Baker, Bernard W. Bell, Donald Gibson. Influential critics of the Black Aesthetic include: Imamu Amiri Baraka, Larry Neal, Addison Gayle, Clarence Major, Hoyt Fuller, Carolyn Rodgers, Sarah Fabio, Ishmael Reed, Cecil Brown, Ed Bullins. Finally there is the group of creative writers who are generally well known and who from time to time have commented on the works of other Afro-American writers. Among these are: James Weldon Johnson, Langston Hughes, Countee Cullen, Wallace Thurman, Richard Wright, Ralph Ellison, James Baldwin, Arna Bontemps, and John Oliver Killens.

The following are significant works published in book form by some of the critics mentioned above:

The New Negro: An Interpretation, Alain Locke, ed. (1925; reissued in paperback)

The Contemporary Negro Novel, Nick Aaron Ford (1936)

The Negro Genius, A New Appraisal of the Achievements of the American Negro in Literature and the Fine Arts, Benjamin Brawley (1937; reissued in paperback)

The Negro in American Fiction and *The Negro in Poetry and Drama*, Sterling Brown (1937; reissued in combined paperback edition)

To Make a Poet Black, Saunders Redding (1939)

Negro Voices in American Fiction, Hugh Gloster (1948)

Notes of a Native Son (1955) and *Nobody Knows My Name* (1961), James Baldwin (Collected personal and critical essays)

Black Fire, Imamu Amiri Baraka and Larry Neal, eds. (1968)

William Wells Brown: Author and Reformer, W. Edward Farrison (1969)

The Militant Black Writer in Africa and the United States, Mercer Cook and Stephen E. Henderson (1969)

Black Expression: Essays by and About Black Americans in the Creative Arts (1969); *The Black Aesthetic* (1971), Addison Gayle, Jr., ed.

Shadow and Act, Ralph Ellison (1964)

The Crisis of the Negro Intellectual, Harold Cruse (1967)[4]

19 Necromancers From Now, Ishmael Reed, ed. (1970)

Five Black Writers: Essays on Wright, Ellison, Baldwin, Hughes and LeRoi Jones, Donald Gibson (1970-71)

In a Minor Chord, Three Afro-American Writers and their Search for Identity, Darwin T. Turner (1971)

Harlem Renaissance, Nathan Huggins (1971)

The Harlem Renaissance Remembered, Arna Bontemps, ed. (1972)

Blackness and the Adventure of Western Culture, George E. Kent (1972)

Long Black Song: Essays in Black American Literature and Culture, Houston A. Baker (1972)

Understanding the New Black Poetry, Stephen E. Henderson (1973)

Relevant Afro-American Periodicals

The Crisis: A Record of the Darker Races, Opportunity: A Journal of Negro Life, and *The Messenger* are periodicals that are particularly helpful in the study of the Harlem Renaissance period. One is still being published monthly: *The Crisis*, organ of the NAACP, began its career in 1910. Its first editor was the eminent W. E. B. DuBois, who commented regularly on the works of black writers and who also had Jessie Fauset on his staff as reviewer and critic. *The Crisis* was an avenue to the public for young black writers of the Renaissance and continues to publish an annual review of literature by Afro-Americans. *Opportunity*, sponsored by the Urban League, was edited by Charles S. Johnson, an entrepreneur of the Renaissance. A monthly journal, published from 1923 to 1946, *Opportunity* included an annual review of literature by and about Afro-Americans, provided opportunities for publication to young black writers and awarded prizes to the best of them—as did *The Crisis*. *Opportunity* also included a column written by the poet Countee Cullen, "The Dark Tower," from 1926 to 1928.

The Messenger, founded in 1917 by A. Philip Randolph and Chandler Owen, claimed to be the "Only Radical Negro Magazine in America." Politically socialist, after its antiwar (World War I) stand, it "joined the elite of American periodicals, those confiscated by the Post Office under suspicion of sedition."[5] *The Messenger* later became the organ of Randolph's Brotherhood of Sleeping Car Porters and continued to publish until 1928 (May-June issue). One of the important Harlem Renaissance figures, acerbic, witty George Schuyler (author of the satiric novel *Black No More*) was actively associated with the magazine, serving in various capacities: contributing editor, managing editor, and assistant editor. Although more political than literary, *The Messenger* also played its part in publicizing the art and literature of the Renaissance, including Claude McKay's "If We Must Die," after it first appeared in the *Liberator* (Max Eastman's magazine).

Phylon: The Atlanta University Review of Race and Culture, was founded in 1940 by W. E. B. DuBois and still publishes quarterly. Lucy Grigsby is currently associate editor; Charles F. Duncan, assistant editor; and Richard A. Long, book reveiw editor. *Phylon* publishes an annual review of literature by and about Afro-Americans, articles of sociological, historical, and literary interest, and a regular feature entitled "Literature of Race and Culture."

The College Language Association was organized in 1939 by a group of black scholars who found the Modern Language Association less than hospitable to their scholarly work. In 1957 they began publishing a journal. Under the able editorial hand of Therman B. O'Daniel at Morgan State College, the *CLA Journal* has published articles concerned with all areas of language and literature, but has always devoted generous space to the criticism of Afro-American writers and their works. Indeed, for a time, although only recently indexed by *PMLA*, *CLA Journal* was one of the few periodicals that consistently published scholarly articles on black literature. Issues have been devoted to individual writers, such as Langston Hughes, Ralph Ellison, James Baldwin, Richard Wright. In 1971, O'Daniel edited *Langston Hughes, Black Genius: A Critical Evaluation* for the Association; this collection of essays included six from the June 1968 issue of *CLA*

Journal dedicated to Hughes.

The *CLA Journal* has always been receptive to both black and white scholars, although it has served as a useful and important forum for the former. *Black World* (formerly *Negro Digest*),[6] a monthly journal, began publishing from 1942 to 1951; then there was a ten-year hiatus in its career until 1961. Hoyt Fuller, as executive editor since 1972, has broadened the coverage from a column on literature by and about Afro-Americans to reviews, critical articles on the discussion and development of black aesthetic concepts, and detailed examinations of the works of individual authors, written almost exclusively by black critics and scholars. Its policy is to encourage the development of young black critics by offering them a forum for their ideas and critical perspectives and rewarding them with prizes of recognition. For example, Geneva Smitherman won the Woodie King, Jr., award for drama criticism for her evaluation of the work of playwright Ed Bullins, "Everybody Wants to Know Why I Sing the Blues," in the April 1974 issue.

Freedomways: A Quarterly of the Negro Freedom Movement has been published since 1961. Associate editors are John Henrik Clarke, Ernest Kaiser and J. H. O'Dell; managing editor, Esther Jackson; contributing editors include Margaret Burroughs, Ruby Dee, and Shirley Graham. Each issue contains an excellent review of recent books by Ernest Kaiser with special attention to works by and about Afro-Americans. The *Liberator* also began publishing in 1961 with Lowell P. Beveridge, Jr., as editor and an editorial board that included James Baldwin and Ossie Davis. The January 1963 editorial reiterated its purpose: "*Liberator* is dedicated to uncompromising participation in the liberation struggle both in America and Africa, thus serving as a bridge for unity between the two movements which must eventually become one." It published history, politics, criticism, some literature (short fiction, poetry—some by Langston Hughes—and essays, by such famous writers as Baldwin), book reviews, and interviews. When *Liberator* ceased publication in 1971, Daniel H. Watts was editor-in-chief, assisted by an editorial staff consisting of Richard Gibson, Clayton Riley (for a time entertainment editor for the *Amsterdam News* and occasional drama reviewer for the *New York Times*) and Tom Feelings.

In 1969 *The Black Scholar: Journal of Black Studies and Research*, *The Journal of Black Poetry*, and *Studies in Black Literature* were launched. *The Black Scholar*, published by Robert Chrisman, is currently edited by Robert Q. Allen. Although it covers a variety of disciplines, the journal always devotes some space to literature, literary criticism, and book reviews. Volume 2 No. 2, January 1971, for example, is devoted entirely to black literature, featuring an unpublished work by Jean Toomer and an extensive article by Lance Jeffers, poet-critic-teacher, entitled

"Afro-American Literature, the Conscience of Man," which examines the fiction of James Weldon Johnson, Richard Wright, James Baldwin, Imamu Baraka in light of Jeffers's thesis, "that black literature as a whole—not the work of occasional authors—is a movement against human wickedness." The April-May 1971 issue featured the writings of black prisoners and the September 1971 issue was dedicated to "Young Black Writers." *The Journal of Black Poetry*, now known as *Kitabu Cha Jua*, is edited by Joe Gonclaves (Dingane); Ed Bullins and Askia Muhammad Touré are editors-at-large; Imamu Baraka, Marvin X, Larry Neal, and Eugene Mkalimoto are contributing editors. *Kitabu Cha Jua*, addressed to "all Black People everywhere," publishes poetry, essays, interviews, criticism, art. Its emphasis is on Africa and the Third World and the cultural influences derived from those non-Western sources. For example, Dr. Ahmed Heikal traces "the impact of Arab Literary Heritage on European Literature" in the Summer 1974 issue. Several issues are guest-edited by black poet-critics Dudley Randall and Don L. Lee. One of the most interesting discussions by Ishmael Reed of his personal literary aesthetic appeared in an early issue (Summer-Fall 1969): "When State Magicians Fail" (Vol. 1, No. 12). *Studies in Black Literature*, edited by Raman K. Singh and published at Mary Washington Colllege in Virginia, accepts work by both black and white scholars and is devoted to critical examination of Afro-American and African literature. All three of these periodicals seem to be alive and in good health.

NOTES

1. All of the works consulted for this study appear in the notes. The two areas of special significance, the slave narrative and criticism by black scholar/critics, are discussed in some detail in this essay.
2. It has also produced a number of workshops and conference sessions. The Institute for Afro-American Culture at the University of Iowa, directed by Darwin T. Turner, devoted its summer session in 1974 to the scholarly examination of the slave narrative.
3. For example, Stephen Henderson is also associated with the Black Aesthetic critics and Addison Gayle is also an academic critic.
4. Cruse is difficult to place in these categories; therefore his name does not appear in any of them. He is currently professor of history at the University of Michigan and is associated with the Department of Afro-American and African Studies.
5. Nathan Huggins, *Harlem Renaissance* (New York, 1971), p. 28.
6. *Black World* is an enterprise of Johnson Publishing Company, which includes *Ebony*, a popular monthly magazine published since 1945 that has a regular "Bookshelf" column. Unfortunately, *Black World* ceased publication in the spring of 1976.

INDEX

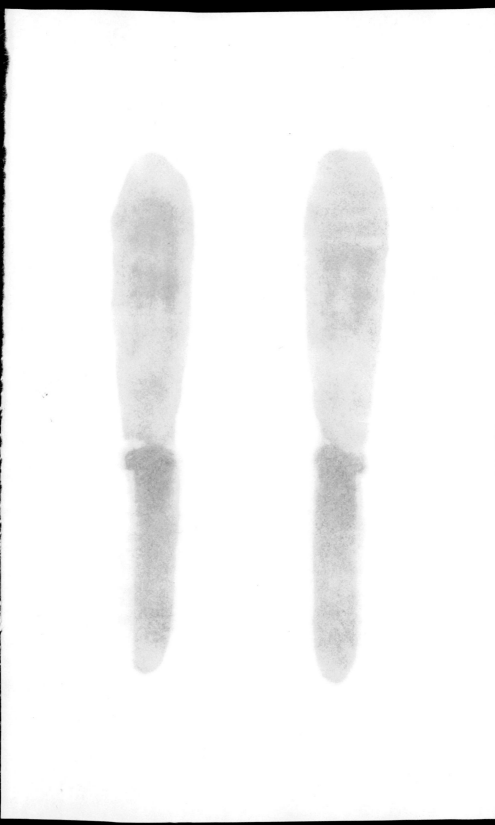